Best Hikes Near
AUSTIN and SAN ANTONIO

"An excellent resource for all who want to explore the outdoors. The color photographs, stories about the area, and hike descriptions, which tell you what to expect on the trail, make it especially suitable for families. This book is informative and fun and inspires you to get outside."
—Chris Holmes, outdoor program coordinator, Texas State Parks

"*Best Hikes Near Austin and San Antonio* is fantastic! I learned new things about hikes I've done over and over. The stories, local history, photos, and maps are great! A well-organized book that will get a lot of use by me and others in our club."
—Bob Cook, president of The Woodlands Hiking Club, The Woodlands, Texas

"*Best Hikes Near Austin and San Antonio* is an excellent hiking guide to thirty trails around this scenic area. Keith weaves stories throughout the book with information about the local history, geology, plant life, wildlife, birds, and more. The trail descriptions are accurate and informative. It is a must-have book for any hiker in Central Texas."
—Robert Stone, author and publisher of hiking guidebooks

Best Hikes Near
Austin and San Antonio

KEITH STELTER

GUILFORD, CONNECTICUT
HELENA, MONTANA

AN IMPRINT OF THE GLOBE PEQUOT PRESS

FALCONGUIDES®

All interior photos by Keith Stelter
Art on page iii © Shutterstock
Text design by Sheryl P. Kober
Maps by Ryan Mitchell © Morris Book Publishing, LLC

Library of Congress Cataloging-in-Publication data is available on file.

ISBN 978-0-7627-4602

Printed in China
10 9 8 7 6 5 4 3 2 1

Contents

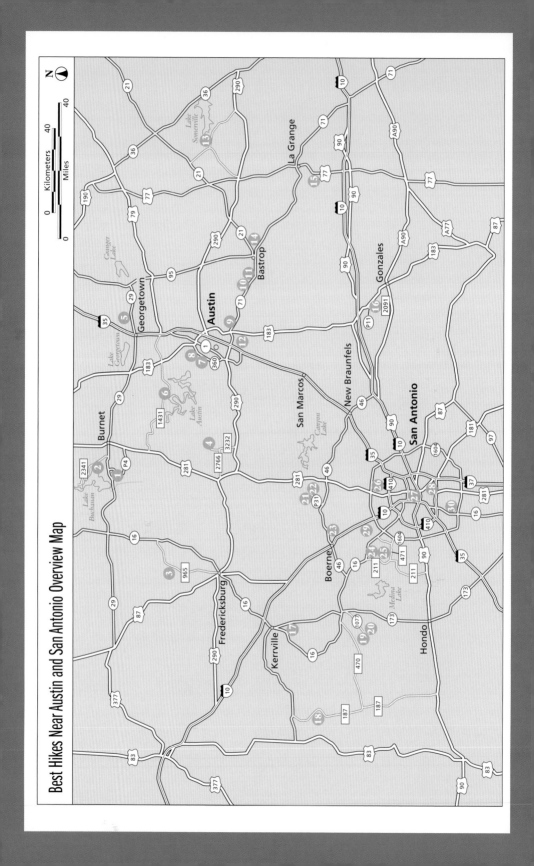

Best Hikes Near Austin and San Antonio Overview Map

Great blue herons are frequently seen around ponds,
streams, and other wet areas.

Acknowledgments

Many people helped make this book possible and a few went "beyond the call of duty." Thanks to Mark, Scott, and Kay Stelter for their encouragement, ideas, and proofreading. Nicole and Jessica Stelter helped with filing and sorting papers. Barbie Miller assisted with proofreading and research. Karen Vasquez with Rick and Samantha Finch went hiking with me.

Thanks also to Chris Holmes, Texas Parks & Wildlife Department (TPWD) regional interpretive specialist, State Parks Region V, for working with me on new trails and the development of Texas Parks and Wildlife trail maps. Bill Beach, TPWD assistant office manager for Guadalupe River State Park, provided me with all kinds of information. Lynn Kuenstler, peace officer at Enchanted Rock State Natural Area, hiked with me and explained vernal pools. There were many other folks at TPWD who were very helpful.

Mike McCracken, site manager, and Karen Gardner, administrative associate at McKinney Roughs Nature Park, part of the Lower Colorado River Authority (LCRA) park system, are due thanks for their assistance. Thanks to Susan Blackledge for help on the Berry Springs Park information. Allison Hardy, GIS technician with the City of Austin Parks and Recreation Department, and Dianne Hart, GIS specialist for San Antonio Natural Areas, helped with making trail maps.

There were dozens of other people who helped with information about history, geology, flora and fauna, and hikes they considered "the best." I appreciate their work and thank all of them.

Acres of wild bluebonnets,
the state flower of Texas, greet travelers in the spring.

Introduction

The purpose of this book is to fill a void. Most hiking guidebooks are slanted toward relatively experienced hikers and the trail descriptions are generally point-to-point guides, getting you safely from the trailhead to the trail's end. The trails selected are good trails, but the books usually cover a single trail at a time. Many lack detail about flora, fauna, history, and geology, which could add a great deal of interest to a broad spectrum of hikers, including families with young children.

To fill these shortcomings I spent nine months researching, talking with rangers and other folks, hiking, and sometimes rehiking a trail, studying the area looking for interesting facts, scenery, history, geology, and topography. I talked with a variety of hikers asking them what they wanted a hike to cover and what made a "best hike." I had the best overall hiking region in Texas to choose from—central Texas, which includes the Edwards Plateau and the Hill Country. I used the following criteria to come up with the best hikes included in this guide: accessibility, fun, exercise, family experience, scenery, history, rivers and lakes, first-time hiker, experienced hiker, moderate length (2 to 7 miles), dog friendly, and wheelchair accessibility. Loops and preferably interconnecting loop trails were selected where possible, so a "best" hike within a park could be fashioned by combining the best of several trails.

Determining the "best" hikes in the area was a combination of personal judgment about who the hike was slanted to and information from park staff and other hikers. Four of my favorite hikes are in the following parks: Lost Maples State Natural Area and Palmetto State Park near San Antonio and Austin's Emma Long City Park and McKinney Roughs Nature Park. The sidebars and In Addition stories that I've included add interesting bits of information about a specific hike or area.

Trails are no longer the exclusive domain of the solitude-loving wilderness seeker or the dedicated fitness enthusiast. Whether providing recreational and educational opportunities, encouraging well-being, exploring history and geology, or bringing together people of all ages, hiking has become an important factor in many people's lives.

I hope that at least some of these hikes will become *your* best hikes and that the book will be informative and interesting reading, as well as an excellent guide.

Austin Weather

The Austin climate is subtropical, with an average low temperature in January of 40°F and an average high in August of 96°F, followed closely by July at 95°F. The average yearly rainfall is 32 inches. The wettest month is May, averaging 5 inches. The driest month is January with 1.9 inches of rain. The city generally has mild temperatures with 300 days of sunshine a year.

Austin Average Monthly Temperature and Precipitation

	Jan	Feb	Mar	Apr	May	June	July	Aug	Sept	Oct	Nov	Dec
Average High	60	65	73	79	85	91	95	96	90	81	70	62
Average Low	40	44	51	58	65	71	73	73	69	60	49	42
Average Precipitation	1.9	2.0	2.1	2.5	5.0	3.8	2.0	2.3	2.9	4.0	2.7	2.4

San Antonio Weather

The San Antonio climate is subtropical, with an average low temperature in January of 39°F and an average high in July and August of 95°F. The average yearly rainfall is 30 inches. The wettest month is May, averaging 4.2 inches. The driest month is March with 1.6 inches of rain, followed closely by January and December with 1.7 inches. The city generally has mild temperatures with 300 days of sunshine a year.

San Antonio Average Monthly Temperature and Precipitation

	Jan	Feb	Mar	Apr	May	June	July	Aug	Sept	Oct	Nov	Dec
Average High	62	66	74	80	86	92	95	95	90	82	71	64
Average Low	39	43	50	58	66	72	74	74	69	59	48	42
Average Precipitation	1.7	1.9	1.6	2.6	4.2	3.6	1.9	2.5	3.2	3.2	2.1	1.7

Current weather and forecasts can be obtained for San Antonio and Austin by calling (830) 606-3617 or the park contact for the hike.

Except for high temperatures and humidity in July and August, and possible showers in May, the weather for hiking in this area is fantastic. A word of caution, the Hill Country is notorious for flash floods—even a few inches of rain can turn shallow streams into raging rivers. Watch the weather and go to high ground if you notice streams rising.

State Parks Pass

For the best deal around, take advantage of the State Parks Pass at an annual cost of $60. Instead of paying on a per person/per visit basis, the pass provides entry to all ninety-three state parks for the member and all occupants of his or her vehicle. It's good for one year from time of purchase.

Flora and Fauna

The hiking trails around Austin and San Antonio, including portions of the Texas Hill Country, have a biodiversity hard to equal. The merging of four major eco-regions—the post oak savanna, the blackland prairie, the south Texas plains, and the Edwards Plateau—is part of the reason. Another is that the Central Flyway, one of four major bird migration routes in the United States, goes directly over

A tufted titmouse sits on a branch,
announcing his presence with a song.

the area. More than 400 of the 600 bird species recorded in the state have been seen in this region. The golden-cheeked warbler and black-capped vireo, both endangered species, are native to Texas. The golden-cheeked warbler nests only in central Texas. Several of the hikes, particularly at Balcones Canyonlands National Wildlife Refuge offer good viewing.

The best indication of birds being present is hearing their songs. The Carolina chickadee sings "chickadee-dee-dee-dee;" the killdeer "kildee, kildee, kildee;" and woodpeckers "rat-atap-rat." The northern mockingbird, the Texas state bird, can be heard mimicking the calls of other birds. Texans claim the mockingbird has the prettiest song of any bird. Some of the most colorful birds include the black-crested titmouse, ladder-backed woodpecker, painted bunting, roadrunner, northern cardinal, eastern bluebird, red-shouldered hawk, great blue heron, and numerous ducks. Millions of Mexican free-tailed bats, the state flying mammal, arrive in central Texas each spring to roost in caves in the Balcones Escarpment and the Edwards Plateau, and are a central attraction under a bridge in Austin.

Most mammals are active during the night, so seeing them can be difficult. Look for their tracks around the trail and near streams or lakes. White-tailed deer, nine-banded armadillos (the state small mammal), coyote, bobcat, beaver, opossum, ring-tailed cat, badger, fox, raccoon, skunk, wild hogs, javelina, fox squirrels, and Rio Grande wild turkeys make their homes here. White-tailed deer are abundant in most of the hiking areas, but are easy to see at Kerrville–Schreiner City Park and Inks Lake State Park. The Houston toad, an endangered species found only in central Texas, breeds in Bastrop State Park.

The Texas Parks & Wildlife Department has developed a series of nature trails including the Great Texas Birding Trail–Central Coast and the Heart of Texas Wildlife Trail–East. Maps and location markers at the various sites reference areas where wildlife may be seen.

Some trees and plants native to east Texas seem to be constantly meeting those of west Texas in transitional zones or isolated pockets. The "Lost Maples" in Lost Maples State Natural Area, the "Lost Pines" in Bastrop State Park, and the dwarf palmettos in Palmetto State Park are examples. Rivers and creeks are lined with bald cypress, black willow, hackberry, sycamore, cottonwood, and pecan. Bald cypress trees add a majestic dimension to waterways, towering up to 120 feet with their cone-shaped "knees" projecting up through the water. Pecan trees, the state tree, also like river shores. The upland areas contain a mix of deciduous and evergreen trees, including Ashe's juniper, live oak, red oak, bigtooth maple, and Texas persimmon. The live oak is an unusual species because it is an evergreen oak tree. Spanish moss can be seen hanging from oaks, bald cypress, and other trees. The Ashe's juniper not only furnishes nesting material for the endangered golden-cheeked warbler, but its berries provide food for berry-foraging wildlife. The Ashe's juniper's blue-black seed cones, known as juniper berries, are used to flavor gin. The most spectacular fall color display in the state is at Lost Maples State Natural Area.

In spring and early summer, when wildflowers set the roadsides ablaze with color, driving to a hiking location can be a visual feast. Commonly seen are coreopsis (yellow), fireweels (red), phlox, Mexican hats, daisies, winecups (purple), yellow primrose, bluestem grass, and prickly pear cactus. The pads and fruit of the prickly pear cactus are edible. The cactus has spectacular red and yellow blooms from early spring to summer. The Texas bluebonnet, the state flower, is at its peak in late March and early April.

The diversity of wildflowers attracts many butterfly species. The monarch, the state insect, is unique among butterflies because of its extremely long migration flight. During the spring and the fall migration, millions of monarchs pass through the area. Guadalupe River State Park, Honey Creek State Natural Area, and Balcones Canyonlands National Wildlife Refuge are excellent locations to see the butterflies.

The great ecological diversity of the territory, along with the flora and fauna, allow trips to be fashioned that are much more than just a "hike in the woods." Enjoy the experience of hiking central Texas.

Wildlife and Bird Viewing Trails

The Texas Parks & Wildlife Department has developed two sets of maps showing prime viewing locations for wildlife and birds. The Heart of Texas Wildlife Trails has an eastern section identified as HOTE and a western section identified as HOTW. The Great Texas Coastal Birding Trail–Central Coast was developed to show premier birding sites. These are identified with a CTC, and there are ninety-five unique sites. Texas was the first state in the nation to create birding and wildlife viewing trails. Some of these sites have viewing blinds. If the possibility of hearing or seeing an endangered species exists, a note identifies the species under the park location.

Golden-cheeked warblers nest only in central Texas. Using these maps can give an added dimension to hiking, including great photo opportunities. More information about these trails and maps, including where to purchase them, can be found at the TPWD Web site www.tpwd.state.tx.us.

In the Austin Area

Park	Site	Hike Number
Bastrop State Park	HOTE 033	14
Endangered species: Houston Toad		
Balcones Canyonland NWR	HOTE 25	6
Endangered species: golden-cheeked warbler		
Monarch butterfly fall migration—October		
Enchanted Rock SNA	HOTW 085	3
McKinney Falls State Park	HOTE 039	12
McKinney Roughs Nature Park	HOTE 034	10, 11
Pedernales Falls State Park	HOTE 050	4

In the San Antonio Area

Park	Site	Hike Number
Cibolo Nature Center	HOTE 078	23
Friedrich Wilderness Park	HOTE 086	29
Endangered species: golden-cheeked warbler		
Guadalupe River SP	HOTW 077	21
Government Canyon SNA	HOTE 085	24, 25
Endangered species: golden-cheeked warbler		
Hill Country SNA	HOTW 045	19, 20
Endangered species: golden-cheeked warbler		
Kerrville-Schreiner Park	HOTW 076	17
Lost Maples SNA	HOTW 061	18
Medina River Park	HOTE 104	30
Mission Espada	HOTE 102	28
Palmetto State Park	CTC 029	16

Zero Impact and Trail Etiquette

We have a responsibility to protect, no longer just conquer and use, our wild places. Many public hiking locations are at risk, so please do what you can to use them wisely. The following section will help you understand better what it means to take care of parks and wild places while still making the most of your hiking experience. Anyone can take a hike, but hiking safely and with good conservation practices is an art requiring preparation and proper equipment.

Always leave an area as good as—or preferably better—than you found it. Key to doing this is staying on the trail. It's true, a path anywhere leads nowhere new, but purists will just have to get over it. Paths serve an important purpose; they limit impact on natural areas. Straying from a designated trail may seem innocent but it can cause damage to sensitive areas—damage that may take areas years to recover from, if they can recover at all. Even simple shortcuts can be destructive. Many of the hikes described in this guide are on or near areas ecologically important to supporting endangered flora and fauna. So, please, stay on the trail.

Leave no weeds. Noxious weeds tend to overtake other plants, which in turn affects animals and birds that depend on them for food. To minimize the spread of noxious weeds, hikers should regularly clean their boots and hiking poles of mud and seeds. Non-native invasive plants are particularly destructive and can quickly destroy acres of habitat. Yaupon is an example. Brush your dog to remove any weed seeds before heading off into a new area.

Keep your dog under control. Always obey leash laws and be sure to bury your dog's waste or pack it in resealable plastic bags.

Respect other trail users. Often you're not the only one on the trail. With the rise in popularity of multiuse trails, you'll have to learn a new kind of respect, beyond the nod and "hello" approach of the past. First investigate whether you're on a multiuse trail, and assume the appropriate precautions. If you hear activity ahead, step off the trail just to be safe.

Mountain bikers can be like stealth airplanes—you may not hear them coming. Be prepared and find out ahead of time whether you share the trail with them. Cyclists should always yield to hikers, but that's little comfort to the hiker. Be aware.

When you approach horses or pack animals on the trail, always step quietly off the trail, preferably on the downhill side, and let them pass.

More trails are being designed to be, at least in part, wheelchair accessible. Always step to the side to allow folks in wheelchairs time to navigate the terrain. Make them aware if you are going to pass around them.

First Aid

Sunburn

Take along sunscreen or sunblock, protective clothing, and a wide-brimmed hat. If you do get a sunburn, protect the area from further sun exposure and treat the area with aloe vera gel or treatment of your choice. Remember that your eyes are vulnerable to damaging radiation as well. Sunglasses can be a good way to prevent eye damage from the sun.

Blisters

Be prepared to take care of these hike-spoilers by carrying moleskin (a lightly padded adhesive), gauze and tape, or adhesive bandages. An effective way to apply moleskin is to cut out a circle of moleskin, remove the center—like a doughnut—and place it over the blistered area. Cutting the center out will reduce the pressure applied to the sensitive skin.

Insect Bites and Stings

You can treat most insect bites and stings by applying hydrocortisone cream (1 percent solution) topically and taking a pain medication of your choice to reduce swelling. If you forgot to pack these items, a cold compress or a paste of mud and ashes can sometimes ease the itching and discomfort. Remove any stingers by using tweezers or scraping the area with your fingernail or a knife blade. Don't pinch the area as you'll only spread the venom.

Some hikers are highly sensitive to bites and stings and may have a serious allergic reaction that can be life threatening. Symptoms of a serious allergic reaction can include wheezing, an asthmatic attack, and shock.

Ticks

Ticks can carry diseases such as Rocky Mountain spotted fever and Lyme disease. The best defense is, of course, prevention. If you know you're going to be hiking through an area containing ticks, wear long pants and a long sleeved shirt. You can apply a permethrin repellent to your clothing and a Deet repellent to exposed skin. At the end of your hike, do a spot check for ticks (and insects in general). If you do find a tick, coat the insect with petroleum jelly or tree sap to cut off its air supply. The tick should release its hold, but if it doesn't, grab the head of the tick firmly—with a pair of tweezers if you have them—and gently pull it away from the skin with a twisting motion. Sometimes the mouth parts linger, embedded in your skin. If this happens, try to remove them with a sterilized needle. Clean the affected area with an antibacterial cleanser and then apply triple-antibiotic ointment. Monitor the area for a few days. If irritation persists or a white spot develops, see a doctor for possible infection.

Poison Ivy, Oak, and Sumac
These skin irritants are prevalent on many of the trails in central Texas, sometimes growing into the trail. They come in the form of a bush or a vine, having leaflets in groups of three (poison ivy and oak), five, seven, or nine. Learn how to spot the plants, and especially show young children what to look for. Poison ivy is the most common found in Texas. Few things can spoil a hike, or your life the week after, than accidentally getting poison ivy. The oil secreted by the plant can cause an allergic reaction in the form of blisters, usually about twelve hours after exposure. The itchy rash can last from ten days to several weeks.

The best defense against these irritants is to wear clothing that covers the arms, legs, and torso. For summer, zip-off cargo pants come in handy. There are also nonprescription lotions you can apply to exposed skin that guard against the effects of poison ivy, oak, or sumac, and can be washed off with soap and water. If you think you were in contact with the plants, after hiking (or even on the trail during longer hikes) wash with soap and water. If the rash spreads, either tough it out or see your doctor.

Natural Hazards
Besides tripping over a rock or tree root on the trail, there are some real hazards to be aware of while hiking, including a few weather conditions and predators you may need to take into account.

Lightning
Thunderstorms build over some areas in central Texas almost every day during the summer. Lightning is generated by thunderheads and can strike without warning, even several miles away from the nearest cloud. The best rule of thumb is to start leaving exposed peaks, ridges, and canyon rims by about noon if the weather forecast includes thunderstorms. This time can vary a little depending on storm buildup. Keep an eye on cloud formation and don't underestimate how fast a storm can build. Lightning takes the path of least resistance, so if you're the high point, it might choose you. Ducking under a rock overhang is dangerous as you form the shortest path between the rock and ground. Avoid having both your hands and feet touching the ground at once and never lay flat. If you hear

a buzzing sound or feel your hair standing on end, move quickly, as an electrical charge is building up.

The National Weather Service provides these cautions;
- If you can hear thunder, you are in striking distance of lightning
- Suspend outdoor activities during thunderstorms and lightning
- Get off high ground
- Do not stay under trees
- Get into an enclosed building or enclosed vehicle

Flash Floods

In July 2007 a torrential downpour (17 inches in twenty-four hours) dumped tons of water into the Marble Falls area near several state parks and hiking trails. Flash flooding, a phenomenon of the Hill Country, flooded trails, homes, and cities, and washed away sections of highways. The spooky thing about flash floods, especially in Hill Country canyons and streambeds, is that they can appear out of nowhere generated by a storm many miles away. While hiking or driving in canyons, keep an eye on the weather. Always climb to safety if danger threatens. Flash floods usually subside quickly, so be patient and don't cross a swollen stream.

Now prepare for your next hike, remembering our responsibilities as modern-day hikers to do our part in conserving the outdoors. Enjoy.

Red-eared slider turtles sun themselves. They splash into the water when they feel vibrations from hikers walking near them.

How to Use This Guide

Each region begins with an introduction, where you're given a sweeping look at the lay of the land. After this general overview, specific hikes within that region are presented. Thirty hikes are detailed in this book.

To aid in quick decision-making, each hike description begins with a hike summary. These short summaries give you a taste of the hiking adventure to follow. You'll learn about the trail terrain and what surprises the route has to offer.

Next you'll find the quick, nitty-gritty details of the hike: where the trailhead is located; hike length; approximate hiking time; difficulty rating; type of trail surface; other trail users; canine compatibility; land status; fees and permits; trail hours; map resources, trail contacts, and other information that will help you on your trek. The **Finding the trailhead** section gives you dependable directions from a nearby city or town right down to where you'll want to park your car.

The hike description is the meat of the chapter. Detailed and honest, it's a carefully researched impression of the trail. While it's impossible to cover everything, you can rest assured that you won't miss what's important.

In the **Miles and Directions** section, mileage cues identify all turns and trail name changes, as well as points of interest. Some hikes end with **Local Information,** which lists resources from which you can learn more about the area.

Don't feel restricted to the routes and trails mapped in this guide. Be adventurous and use the book as a platform to discover new routes for yourself. One of the simplest ways to begin is to turn the map upside down and hike the trail in reverse. The change in perspective can make the hike feel quite different; it's like getting two hikes for one.

You may wish to copy the directions for the course onto a small sheet to help you while hiking, or photocopy the map and cue sheet to take with you. Otherwise, just slip the whole book in your backpack and take it with you. Enjoy your time in the outdoors and remember to pack out what you pack in.

You will find Green Tips scattered throughout the guide. These are offered as suggestions for ways to reduce your impact both on the trails and on the planet.

How to Use the Maps

Overview Map: This map (see page vi) shows the location of each hike in the area by hike number. It is keyed to the table of contents.

Route Map: This is your primary guide to each hike. It shows all of the accessible roads and trails, points of interest, access to water, towns, landmarks, and geographical features. It also distinguishes trails from roads, and paved roads from unpaved roads. The selected route is highlighted, and directional arrows point the way.

Legend

Roads

- Freeway/Interstate Highway
- U.S. Highway
- State Highway
- Other Road
- Unpaved Road

Trails

- Selected Route
- Trail or Fire Road
- Paved Trail or Bike Path
- Steps
- Direction of Travel

Water Features

- Body of Water
- River or Creek
- Intermittent Stream
- Marsh or Wetland

Land Management

- Parks and Preserves
- Watersheds

Map Symbols

- Trailhead
- Picnic Area
- Visitor Center/Information
- Parking
- Restroom
- Telephone
- Water
- Campground
- Gate
- Mountain/Peak
- Building/Point of Interest
- Scenic View
- Interpretive Panel
- True North (Magnetic North is approximately 15.5° East)

Trail Finder

Hike No.	Hike Name	Best Hikes for Families and Children	Best Hikes for Great Views	Best Hikes for Lake Lovers	Best Hikes for River Lovers	Best Hikes for Canyons	Best Hikes for Geology Lovers	Best Hikes for History Lovers	Best Hikes for Nature Lovers, including Bird-Watchers	Best Hikes for Dogs	Best Hikes for Physically Challenged
1	Pecan Flats and Green Trails	●		●			●		●		●
2	Beebrush Loop			●					●	●	
3	Summit Trail		●				●	●	●		
4	Wolf Mountain Trail		●			●			●	●	
5	Muy Grande	●						●	●	●	●
6	Cactus Rocks Trail								●		
7	Turkey Creek Trail								●	●	
8	Hill and Creek Trails								●		
9	Primitive Trail								●		
10	Riverside Trails		●		●	●	●		●		●
11	Buckeye Trail								●		
12	Homestead Trail				●		●	●	●		
13	Flag Pond Loop								●	●	
14	Lost Pines and Scenic Overlook Trails							●	●	●	
15	Scenic and Historic Trails	●						●			●

Trail Finder

#	Trail											
16	Palmetto, Hiking, and Lake Trails	•		•	•		•		•		•	•
17	Red, Green, Orange Trails			•	•		•		•			
18	East Trail		•	•	•	•	•		•			
19	Hermit's Trace		•			•	•		•	•		
20	Wilderness and Twin Peaks Trails						•	•	•	•		
21	Loops 2 and 3				•		•		•	•		
22	Honey Creek Interpretive Trail	•						•	•			
23	Prairie, Creekside, and Woodlands Trails	•			•		•	•	•	•		
24	Savannah Loop		•				•	•	•		•	
25	Bluff Spurs					•			•			
26	McAllister Park Loop	•				•			•	•		•
27	Paseo del Rio	•			•			•		•		•
28	Mission Espada							•				
29	Main Loop, Vista Loop, and Fern Del Trail		•			•	•		•		•	
30	El Camino and Rio Medina Trails				•				•			•

Migrating waterfowl pass across the rising sun, heading toward feeding gounds.

Austin, the state capital and geographical center of Texas, is at the intersection of Interstate 35 and U.S. Highways 183 and 290 and is 70 miles northeast of San Antonio. It is a gateway to the Hill Country on the west and the Highland Lakes on the north. A series of dams on the Colorado River have created an extraordinary 150-mile chain of seven lakes, offering good hiking opportunities at Inks Lake State Park and the Canyon of the Eagles.

About forty million years ago, a fault zone spawned the Balcones Escarpment, which runs through the western half of the city and down through San Antonio. This uplift formed two physically unique areas. The Balcones Canyonlands (Warbler Vista, Government Canyon State Natural Area, and Friedrich Wilderness Park), a limestone plateau of deeply eroded, steep, rocky hills is on the west, and the Blackland Prairie, with its rolling hills overlooking wide valleys, is on the east. The hills (some Texans longingly call them mountains) range from less than 100 feet above sea level to over 2,000 feet. Austin sits on top of the Edwards Plateau, a very large elevated section of land that lies along the fault.

Pilot Knob volcano erupted 70 million years ago near what is now McKinney Falls State Park. As volcanic activity ceased, beaches developed around the volcanic ash mound. One such beach is along Onion Creek, which is responsible for both Upper and Lower McKinney Falls (Homestead Trail). As the shallow oceans around the volcanoes subsided, erosion created hills and valleys. The small peaks seen from the trails around the box canyons of McKinney Roughs Nature Park, are called "knobs" and are made up of the remains of large oyster beds.

Pink granite is unusual in Central Texas. Only Inks Lake State Park and Enchanted Rock State Natural Area have trails that include domes of granite interspersed with pink.

This rich history of geological events has created an area where hikers can choose flat lakeside lowland hikes (Canyon of the Eagles and Nails Creek State Park), hikes through wide valleys, rolling grassy hills, and steep limestone and granite outcroppings (Inks Lake State Park and Friedrich Wilderness Park), hikes along rivers flowing past towering limestone bluffs (Guadalupe River State Park) and treks among a variety of other physical features to satisfy any particular want. Unique to the region is the thrusting up of pink granite through black limestone to make spectacular hiking at Enchanted Rock State Natural Area. This shared geology is the glue that holds Austin, San Antonio, and the adjoining Hill Country together to make it great hiking country.

Austinites enjoy mild temperatures and 300 days of sunshine a year, and are known for their love of the outdoors. In 1827 Stephen F. Austin was granted land by the Mexican government for his third colony, which included Waterloo. The nearby Colorado River became a magnet for settlers. Waterloo was renamed Austin in 1839 and became the capital of the Republic of Texas. In 1842 invading Mexican troops captured San Antonio, and Houston was temporarily made the capital. The Republic of Texas joined the United States of America in 1845, and Austin was selected the temporary capital; it did not become the permanent capital of Texas until 1872.

A mother and daughter rest at McKinney Falls.

Inks Lake State Park: Pecan Flats and Green Trails

The Pecan Flats Trail (wheelchair accessible) and the rugged Green Trail travel through live oak, mountain juniper woodlands, across rock debris fields and over steep granite domes, and above the Inks Lake shoreline. Sometimes the trail disappears on the rock surface, as outcroppings of pink granite jut up through the limestone. In spring, vernal pools form in rock depressions, only to disappear by midsummer. The pools regenerate the next year. Does with fawns can be seen in Pecan Flats among the Ashe's junipers and prickly pear cactus. The view looking down from the domes of the 803-acre Inks Lake is inspiring.

Start: Pecan Flats trailhead on Park Road 4

Nearest town: Burnet

Distance: 3 miles; interconnecting lollipops

Approximate hiking time: 1 hour (Pecan Flats Trail); 1.25 hours (Green Trail)

Difficulty: Easy (wheelchair accessible) for the Pecan Flats Trail; moderate for the Green Trail, due to the up-and-down over granite

Trail surface: Crushed granite, dirt, sand, granite

Seasons: September to June

Other trail users: Dog walkers

Canine compatibility: Leashed dogs permitted

Land status: State park; Texas Parks and Wildlife Department

Fees and permits: $4 per person 13 years of age and older. Texas residents 65 or older pay $2 each. Or use the State Parks Pass.

Schedule: 8:00 a.m. to 10:00 p.m. daily

Maps: Inks Lake trail maps are available in the park office. You can also find maps on the Web site www.tpwd.state.tx.us.

Trail contacts: Inks Lake State Park, 3630 Park Road 4 West, Burnet, TX 78611; (512) 793-2223

Other: Public hunts take place during the first weeks in December and January, when the park is closed to the general public. Call (512) 793-2223 for specific dates.

Finding the trailhead:
From Austin, take Highway 183 north to Highway 29, and go west 9 miles to Burnet. Turn left onto Park Road 4 and proceed 3 miles to the park headquarters—at 3630 PR 4. Pecan Flats Trail is a short drive from park headquarters. As you leave headquarters, turn right on PR 4 and follow it to the parking area marked CAMPING AND AMPHITHEATER PARKING ONLY. The trailhead is across PR 4, about 0.3 mile northwest of the parking lot. DeLorme's *Texas Atlas & Gazetteer:* Page 69 B7. GPS: N30° 43' 850" W98° 22' 220"

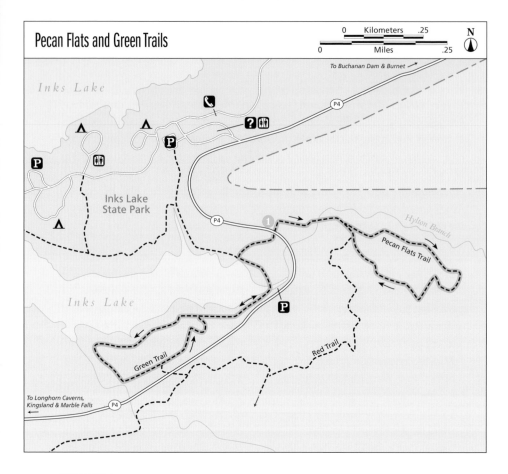

To Buchanan Dam & Burnet

Inks Lake

P4

Inks Lake
State Park

P4

Hylton Branch

Pecan Flats Trail

Inks Lake

P

Red Trail

Green Trail

To Longhorn Caverns,
Kingsland & Marble Falls

P4

THE HIKE

This hike combines the Pecan Flats Trail and the considerably more difficult Green Trail. In the spring and early summer, white-tailed deer with their white-spotted fawns can be seen grazing at the trail's edge. Pick up a Pecan Flats Trail guide at the park office. This interpretive guide describes the unusual geology, flora, and fauna found here.

Start on the Pecan Flats Trail from the parking area marked CAMPING AND AMPHI-THEATER PARKING ONLY. Follow the trail east and then head south. Continue following the loop clockwise, walking around the Ashe's junipers (Texans call them cedars). Benches are placed conveniently along the trail and are usually in shaded places.

Small sunny clearings among the trees allow black-eyed Susans and prickly pear cactus, which is the state plant of Texas, to flourish. Large pieces of granite, many rectangular-shaped, are along the trail. A tall yucca plant near some large boulders is on the right, close to marker 23. Native Americans wove baskets and made sandals from the fibers in its leaves. The yucca is also known as the Spanish dagger. Cross over a seasonal streambed, which has flowing water only after a rain. There is a cedar log bench near the branch connecting the ends of the Pecan Flats Trail loop.

Veer hard left, changing direction from east to north and going around cedars, cactus, and grass. Go through an area about 100 feet long where concrete blocks border both sides of the trail. Pass a number of markers that are not in numerical order but that relate to the interpretive guide. Then zigzag a bit, passing granite outcrops along the trail edge. Small clearings allow glimpses of the surrounding hills. Just before you complete the loop, you'll pass the Red Trail on the left. Continue on the Pecan Flats Trail, following the left (northwest) trail back toward the start.

Continue to the trailhead and take the connector path west to the Green Trail. Where the connector forms a T with the Green Trail, turn left (east), with the lake on your right. There are no benches on the Green Trail, but plenty of rocks to sit on. The trail winds through cedar forest along the lake's edge, across rock-strewn debris fields, and then heads up the granite hills. At the beginning of the loop, bear right to head west along the lake shore, going up the granite domes.

Lichens cover much of the pink granite, giving it a black or green appearance. The pink outcrops jutting up through the limestone are Valley Spring gneiss

Look down on Inks Lake from atop a pink granite dome on the Green Trail. Vernal pools may also be found on the granite.

("nice"), from the Precambrian era, and are part of the Llano Uplift. Feldspar minerals in the rock glitter in the sun. Enchanted Rock State Natural Area is the only other park where pink granite is found. Look for small, temporary rainwater basins called vernal pools that support a variety of plants. The water evaporates by midsummer and regenerates with the next spring rain. Dry gravelly areas and shaded crevices support a diversity of wildflowers, wild onions, grasses, mosses, lichens, and ferns. The trail disappears and reappears on the surface of the solid granite as it continues up onto the domes. Generally, going straight ahead or to the left keeps you on the trail. On the top, the 360-degree views covering the 803-acre lake and surrounding hills are inspiring. The top is bare, except for a few cactus and scattered grasses. There are some steep sections both going up to the domes and coming down.

Head down away from the lake to the completion of the loop. Take the right (east) branch and backtrack to the trailhead. The park also has several miles of other trails.

MILES AND DIRECTIONS

0.0 Start at the Pecan Flats trailhead. It is about 0.3 mile from the parking area to the trailhead.

0.4 The trail, which had been heading southeast, now makes a sharp bend right, heading south.

0.6 After making a sweeping right turn heading generally north, and then a sharp left turn heading south, make a hard right heading northwest.

1.0 Pass the branch to the Red Trail. It is on the left side and heads southwest. Continue on the Pecan Flats Trail loop past where the loop connects to itself. Go through the parking area and cross PR 4, following the connector west to the Green Trail.

1.5 Reach the T intersection with the Green Trail. Follow the left branch heading east. Inks Lake is on the right, and the trail parallels the south side of the lake. The trail generally bears right.

1.8 Continue straight, past where the loop section of the Green Trail intersects on the left (south) side to follow the loop counterclockwise. The lake is still on the right, and the trail follows its edge closely.

2.1   The trail bends sharply left (southeast), and the climb to the domes begins.

2.2   Pass a connector on the right that leads to the Red Trail. Continue walking on the domes. There are good views of the lake, which is now on the left (north).

2.7   Reach the T that connects the loop. Take the right (east) branch and backtrack.

3.0   The connector trail intersecting the Green Trail is on the right (north). Take the connector trail and continue backtracking. Cross PR 4 to the parking area.

The Texas state house was constructed using pink granite.

Bullfrogs can often be heard and seen along pond edges near trails.

Canyon of the Eagles: Beebrush Loop

This hike offers solitude and the opportunity to explore nearly pristine countryside. Lake lovers will enjoy hiking the flat lowlands along the eastern shoreline of Lake Buchanan. The entire west side of Canyon of the Eagles borders the lake. Armadillos and wild hogs are common. Bald eagles may be seen November through March in the tall trees around the lake. In spring a profusion of wildflowers and prickly pear cactus blooms. A series of complex, well-marked loops in this 940-acre park allows you to alter your route on the go.

Start: Beebrush Trail trailhead

Nearest town: Burnet

Distance: 2.9 miles; interconnecting loops

Approximate hiking time: 1.5 hours

Difficulty: Easy, due to the flat surface

Trail surface: Crushed gravel, dirt, grass

Seasons: September to June

Other trail users: Dog walkers

Canine compatibility: Leashed dogs permitted

Land status: Lower Colorado River Authority preserve

Fees and permits: $5 per day. Day use only.

Schedule: 8:00 a.m. to 5:00 p.m. daily

Maps: Trail maps are available in the lodge office and on the Web site www.lcra.org.

Trail Contacts: Canyon of the Eagles Nature Park, Highway 2341 NE, Lake Buchanan, Burnet, TX, 78611; (512) 369-4780

Other: Some trails are closed November 1 through March 15 to protect bald eagles, and from March 1 to August 1 to protect the endangered golden-cheeked warbler.

Finding the trailhead:

Canyon of the Eagles is about 1 hour and 15 minutes northwest of Austin. From the capital, take Interstate 35 north to Georgetown. Exit onto Highway 29 to Burnet (exit 261) and turn left at the light to get onto Highway 29 west. Continue on Highway 29 through Burnet. Turn right onto Ranch Road 2341; there will be a sign for Canyon of the Eagles at that turnoff. Follow RR 2341 for 15 miles until the road dead-ends at the front entrance gate. Proceed to the lodge office to get a map. Then drive to the Amphitheater parking lot and Beebrush Trail trailhead. DeLorme's *Texas Atlas & Gazetteer*: Page 68 J5. GPS: N30° 52' 871" W98° 26' 278"

View Lake Buchanan from the Lakeside Trail in Canyon of the Eagles preserve. Lake Buchanan is one of seven connecting lakes west of Austin.

THE HIKE

Start on Beebrush Loop at marker 3, in Canyon of the Eagles Nature Park. The terrain is flat, and prickly pear cactus, the state plant, is abundant. Sections of three trails—Beebrush Loop, Rocky Point Trail, and Lakeside Trail—have been combined to show the best of the shoreline, lowlands, and hills, and to offer opportunities to see the flora and fauna on the west side of the preserve.

Many of the trails in the park are interconnecting loops, so simple adjustments can be made to shorten, lengthen, or change directions while hiking. This makes the hike suitable for most ages and experience levels. The trail intersections on the map are numbered 1 through 28, and the physical trail markers have the same numbers. It's common to see lizards, some up to 10 inches long, scurrying across the path. Towering live oak, cedar trees, and a variety of shrubs line both sides of the trail.

Continue veering left on Beebrush Loop to the intersection with Rocky Point Trail. Keep straight, heading west on Rocky Point Trail for a short distance to Tanner Point, where you will find an 8-foot-long wooden viewing platform overlooking a large bay of Lake Buchanan. The lake was created by damming the Colorado River and is one of seven Highland lakes.

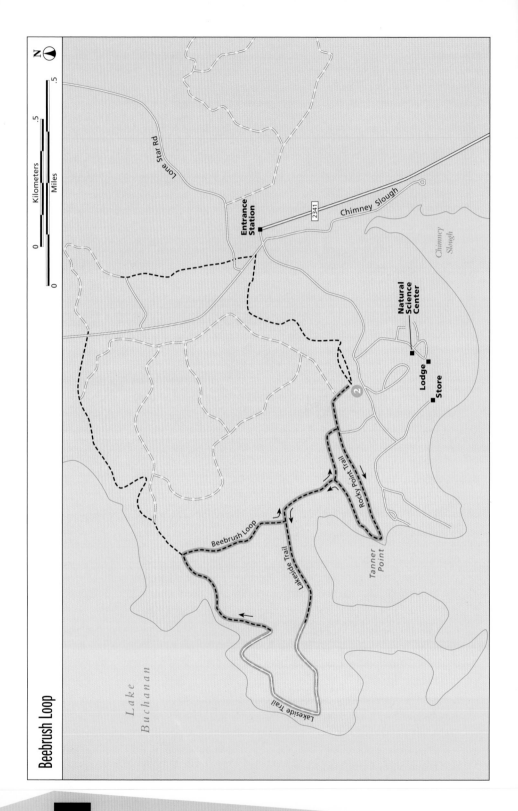

Beebrush Loop

Bend hard right, almost reversing directions, and heading east, following the shoreline. The trail goes slightly uphill and leads away from the lake. Be alert for a T intersection as there are many. The lake comes in and out of sight, due to the terrain and vegetation. Much of this hike is in open canopy, so bring plenty of water.

A narrow path on the right leads away from the trail to a scenic overlook of the valley. The view, with its many trees and colorful flowers, including black-eyed Susans, is worth the time to visit. There are numerous places along the trail where white-tailed deer have bedded down in the tall grass. Look for spots where the grass has been laid over and for deer tracks on the trail. White-tailed deer, armadillos, and wild hogs are frequently seen. Most of the park's 940 acres have been set aside as a nature preserve and habitat for the endangered golden-cheeked warbler and black-capped vireo and the majestic bald eagle.

Continue through several intersections and branches to the Lakeside Trail, a path that makes a loop near the lake's edge. Dragonflies, including green darters, and grasshoppers are abundant.

Trail sections between markers 8 to 9 and 9 to 10 are closed from November 1 through March 15 to protect bald eagles. But this is the best place to view the lake and also, at marker 8, to get a glimpse of bald eagles sitting in trees around the water's edge.

At some points the trail is narrow and overgrown with wild grass. Limestone outcroppings come to the edge, with prickly pear cactus appearing to grow from the cracks in the rocks. Continue past an intersection on the right and the next section should be familiar, since it was used earlier in the hike.

Backtrack the short distance to the trailhead. The numerous intersections and branches may sound confusing, but since the trails are well marked, they just add a bit of interest to the hike.

There are 14 miles of trails in the park, but 7 miles of trails on the east side are closed from March through August, during the golden-cheeked warbler nesting period. The park also has 3 miles of wheelchair-accessible paths.

MILES AND DIRECTIONS

Note: All trail markers are shown on the Canyon of Eagles map.

0.0 Start at the Beebrush trailhead.

0.1 At trail marker 3 bear left (west), heading toward Rocky Point Trail.

0.2 At trail marker 4 take the left branch, which is Rocky Point Trail and leads to trail marker 5.

0.5 Trail marker 5 is located at Tanner Point. Lake Buchanan is to the west. Follow the trail hard right, heading east toward trail marker 6.

0.7 Beebrush Loop intersects Rocky Point Trail at trail marker 6. Head north on Beebrush Loop toward trail marker 7.

0.9 At trail marker 7, Lakeside Trail intersects Beebrush Loop. Turn left onto Lakeside Trail, heading west and toward trail marker 8.

1.2 At trail marker 8 there is a Y branch where a small loop of the trail connects to itself. Stay left, heading west toward trail marker 9. *Note:* From November 1 through March 15, the section of trail between markers 8 and 10 is closed to protect bald eagles. Go right (north) from trail marker 8 directly to trail marker 10 during this period.

1.4 At trail marker 9 veer right, heading north and following the lakeshore toward trail marker 10.

1.8 At trail marker 10, this loop of the Lakeside Trail joins the main trail. Bear left, going north toward trail marker 11.

2.1 The trail branches at trail marker 11. Turn right (south) onto the Beebrush Loop trail, heading toward trail marker 7. We've been here before.

2.4 The Beebrush Loop intersects with Lakeside Trail at trail marker 7. Continue going south, heading toward trail marker 6.

2.6 At trail marker 6 veer left (east) toward trail marker 4.

2.7 At trail marker 4 turn left, heading west toward trail marker 3. From here backtrack to the trailhead and parking lot.

2.9 End the hike at trail marker 3 and the trailhead.

When it was built, Buchanan Dam was the longest multiple-arch dam in the United States, with a length of just over 2 miles. The dam impounded the Colorado River to create Lake Buchanan. Native Americans who once lived in the Canyon of the Eagles area considered it sacred ground. Over 30,000 artifacts were found when the Buchanan Dam and lake were being built in the 1930s.

Enchanted Rock State Natural Area: Summit Trail

Scrambling up a solid pink granite dome, skirting boulder fields, and avoiding large-scale dropoffs—while experiencing an elevation rise of 425 feet in half a mile—make this an incredible hike. You'll see vernal pools that have taken thousands of years to form. As an added adventure, Enchanted Rock cave, a deep, narrow, covered ravine, lies about 150 yards north of the summit. Only Stone Mountain in Georgia is a larger batholith (granite dome). Enchanted Rock was designated a National Natural Landmark by the U.S. Department of the Interior in 1971 and in 1984 was included in the National Register of Historic Places.

Start: At the gazebo next to the parking lot
Nearest town: Fredericksburg
Distance: 1.4 miles out-and-back
Approximate hiking time: 1 hour
Difficulty: Strenuous, due to a 425-foot rise in elevation in 0.6 mile over solid granite
Trail surface: Some gravel, then solid granite
Seasons: September to June
Other trail users: Dog walkers
Canine compatibility: Leashed dogs permitted
Land status: State Park Natural Area; Texas Parks & Wildlife Department
Fees and permits: $5 per person or use the State Parks Pass.
Schedule: 8:00 a.m. to 10:00 p.m.

daily, except during public hunts. When the park reaches parking capacity (usually on weekends, holidays, and during spring break), it will close temporarily, opening again in the evening.
Maps: The Enchanted Rock trail map is available in the park office or on the Web site www.tpwd.state.tx.us.
Trail contacts: Enchanted Rock State Natural Area, 16710 Ranch Road 965, Fredericksburg, TX 78624; (830) 685-3636; www.tpwd.state.tx.us
Other: Public hunts are normally scheduled during the first two weeks in January, at which time the park is closed to the general public. Call ahead for specific dates.

Finding the trailhead:
From Austin take U.S. Highway 290 west to Fredericksburg. A few blocks west of the courthouse in Fredericksburg, take Ranch Road 965 north (right). Enchanted Rock is about 18 miles ahead, with the entrance on the left. Check in at the park headquarters. The trailhead is near the gazebo next to the parking lot. DeLorme's *Texas Atlas & Gazetteer:* Page 68 D4. GPS: N30° 30' 348" W98° 49' 086"

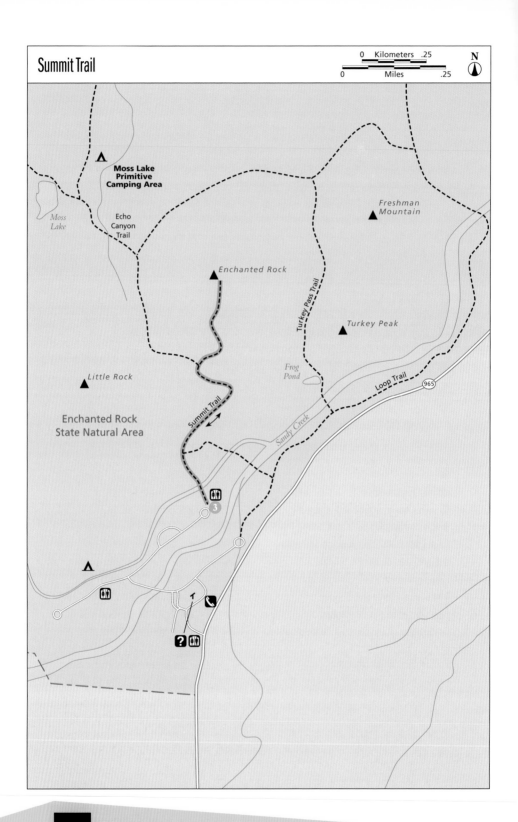

THE HIKE

Steep stairs with about fifty steps lead down from the gazebo to the base of Enchanted Rock. Bear right to Summit Trail, which has a surface of crushed gravel. Pass a small bench shaded by a live oak tree on the left, then go over a rocky granite outcrop and cross a shallow seasonal stream. Depending on the season, prickly pear cactus (the state plant), fairy sword ferns, grasses, and wildflowers may be blooming.

Climb the steps, which were built by park volunteers. The small pieces of pink granite around them are called *grus*. Skirt around some small boulder fields and continue straight ahead between blocks of granite that cross the trail. Several of the rocks are mushroom-shaped and are called mushroom rocks.

The trail gets steeper and disappears on the bare granite slope. Watch for small circular depressions with rounded, raised rims; these are called rock doughnuts. They can be from 1 inch to 10 feet in height. Sounds like Fred Flintstone could have breakfast here.

Farther up the trail on the left are two granite slabs: The largest is about 8 feet high and 20 feet long. The climb is steep, a 425-foot rise in elevation in about half a mile. On the right (northeast), Turkey Peak, Freshman Mountain, and Buzzard's Roost dominate the view. Turkey vultures are conspicuous as they ride thermal air currents.

Much of the pink surface of the granite has been covered by lichens, appearing to change its color to predominantly black with patches of yellow, orange, and green. Numerous depressions are visible in the granite, the largest being about 30

Vernal pools form when water collects in depressions in rocks.
They can be lush with vegetation in the spring.

Little Rock Dome displays a great example of rock exfoliation,
where large slabs of granite separate from a dome.

feet across and 18 inches deep. Before they accumulate soil and hold water, these
weathered pits are called *gnammas*. Those holding water become vernal pools.
The best examples are near the top, where the dome flattens. Some, like an oasis in
the desert, turn into pockets of vegetation. Look for fairy shrimp, which are indig-
enous to these pools. They are ½- to 1½-inches long. Their colors range from red-
orange to ghostly translucent whitish, blue, or green. These pools are very fragile
micro-ecosystems. Do not walk in them or disturb them.

The summit is not a peak, but merely the highest point of the nearly flat dome.
A round bronze Coast and Geodetic survey marker is embedded there. To locate
the marker, walk to the center of the summit, then head west toward Little Rock.
Little Rock has excellent examples of granite slabs in the process of exfoliating, or
"sheeting off." To the east is a long hill with a flat top that is a small section of the
Edwards Plateau. Be careful, there are 80-foot dropoffs at the edge of the summit.

The Tonkawa and Comanche Indians treated the rock as holy ground
because they believed ghost fires flickered at the top. They often heard weird
creaking sounds, which they thought were evil spirits roaming about. Geologists
report that the rock's heating by day and contracting in the cool night caused
the sounds.

About 150 yards north, across the summit and slightly down, lies Enchanted
Rock cave. A flashlight is needed to explore it. In the summer snakes and spiders
use the cave for shade.

*In Texas for a space to be called a cave, a human must be able
to enter it for a distance of 15 feet in length and/or depth.*

From this point backtrack to the trailhead, keeping the gazebo in view while backtracking. Things look different going down, and folks have made wrong turns and required rescue.

The park has 7 miles of other trails, including a loop trail that joins Summit Trail. Because the parking lot often reaches capacity and frequently closes as early as 11 a.m. on weekends, it is wise to call ahead.

MILES AND DIRECTIONS

0.0 Start at the Summit trailhead at the gazebo adjacent to the parking area. Go down the steps and continue heading north.

0.1 Pass a bench on the left. Straight ahead is the summit trail marker on the left and the loop trail marker on the right. Follow the Summit Trail, then bear right as it goes over some granite outcrop.

0.2 Cross over a small seasonal stream. Go up some rocky granite "steps" past a summit trail marker.

0.3 Pass a trail marker with an arrow pointing in the trail direction. At first you're still on the "steps," then the trail turns to solid granite. Continue generally heading north.

0.4 Pass by large rocks and several large blocks of granite (8 feet high and 20 feet long).

0.5 Pass by some more large boulders and a vernal pool supporting some grasses and cactus.

0.6 Look to the right (east) to view Turkey Peak dome.

0.7 Pass some vernal pools (they dry out in summer) and reach the summit of Enchanted Rock. The summit is generally flat. Then continue north about 150 yards to Enchanted Rock cave. The cave is very close to the edge of the summit. Backtrack to the trailhead.

1.4 End at the trailhead at the gazebo.

Fairy Shrimp in Vernal Pools

Fairy shrimp living in vernal pools sounds like a line from a science fiction story. This is what I thought a few years ago when I first visited Enchanted Rock and a ranger offered to hike up the rock with me and find some of these crustaceans.

▶

Summit Trail

Not having any idea of what a vernal pool was, I asked the ranger. He replied, "Since 'vernal' means appearing in spring, it should be pretty obvious." Great, now we had magical pools appearing on solid rock in the spring! Reluctantly, I asked how shrimp could live on this solid granite rock we were scrambling up. His answer was that he would show me when we found a pool. On top of getting winded, I was becoming skeptical and hoping he wasn't taking me on one of those "Let's find the snipe" hikes that I had been led on as a boy!

We were getting closer to the top and he pointed at several small empty depressions and said they had been vernal pools. These depressions are formed when the rock becomes abraded and the wear continues for very long periods of time. The basins collect water from rain in the spring and dry out by summer, leaving some dirt, possibly containing eggs from the fairy shrimp. They refill the following spring.

The ranger passed a shallow depression in the granite and then reached a pool about 10 feet in diameter and less than 2 feet deep. He got down on one knee to better observe the shallow pool and told me the pools can be from 1 foot to larger than 20 feet in diameter. Plant life and a small shrub were growing in it, making it resemble an oasis in the desert.

The ranger told me to get down on all fours to see the shrimp. I noticed several hikers had stopped to see what we were doing. I got down alongside the pool, looked into it, and even though the water was clear, could see nothing. I thought, "Here it comes, I'm going to be 'sniped.'" But he continued observing and told me to look for an almost transparent, shrimp-like thing, about ½- to 1½-inches long, swimming upside down and having eleven legs. Still no luck. He told me they might be red-orange or even whitish, depending on the food supply in the pool. Then, a smile came to his face, he had spotted several and pointed to where I should look. One was drifting slowly and several were darting about. They were not easy to spot. Sweet success and no embarrassing snipe hunt.

Then, putting his hand gently in the water, the ranger removed some debris that a careless hiker had thrown in the pool. These pools are very fragile ecosystems; they have taken hundreds of years and even longer to develop. Putting items in them, removing water from them, or stepping in them can destroy the entire system.

On the hike back down, the ranger said one reason these shrimp have survived is that the female produces two types of eggs. One is a thin-shelled quick-to-hatch "summer" egg and the other is a thick-shelled "winter" egg that remains in the dirt and hatches when the depression refills with water in the spring. He went on to say that since the shrimp live in a temporary wetland (now that's a real stretch—a depression in a piece of rock has become a wetland!) there are no predatory fish.

The hike had been a success, fairy shrimp really did live in vernal pools, and I had a lot of fun with the ranger. Vernal pools can also be seen in the granite outcroppings at Inks Lake State Park.

Pedernales Falls State Park: Wolf Mountain Trail

The Wolf Mountain Trail is a Hill Country classic. Pass through scrubland, dense cedar woodlands, and valley vistas while wrapping around Wolf Mountain. Wind along the small canyons created by Mescal and Tobacco Creeks, with stunning views of the Pedernales River valley. Cross Bee Creek, a small seasonal creek, and look to the left for views of the steep canyon walls that line the creek. The water cascading over the limestone creek bottom adds a special touch. The trail has a number of short spurs that reach the bluffs overlooking the creeks. Dogs love this park.

Start: Wolf Mountain Trail parking area

Nearest town: Johnson City

Distance: 3.8 miles out-and-back

Approximate hiking time: 2.5 hours

Difficulty: Moderate, due to long inclines and some steep grades going around Wolf Mountain

Trail surface: Packed gravel

Seasons: September to June

Other trail users: Mountain bikers, dog walkers

Canine compatibility: Leashed dogs permitted

Land status: State park; Texas Parks & Wildlife Department

Fees and permits: $4 per person, or you can use the State Parks Pass.

Schedule: 8:00 a.m. to 10:00 p.m. daily

Maps: Ask at the park office or visit the Web site www.tpwd.state.tx.us.

Trail contacts: Pedernales Falls State Park, 2585 Park Road 6026, Johnson City, TX 78636; (830) 868-7304

Other: *Warning!* The Pedernales River runs through the park and can flash flood with little or no warning. The water can rise from a shallow stream to a raging torrent in a few minutes. If you are in the area and notice the water beginning to rise, leave *immediately.* Flash flooding is common in the Texas Hill Country. Be alert to weather conditions.

Finding the trailhead:
From Austin head west on U.S. Highway 290. Go about 30 miles and turn north on Farm Road 3232. Continue north for 6 miles, until FM 3232 dead-ends at a T in the road. The entrance to Pedernales Falls State Park is at the junction with Farm Road 2766, at 2585 Park Road 6026. Drive north less than 3 miles to park headquarters. From there, take the park road west to the first intersection and turn right (south) to the Wolf Mountain Trail parking area. DeLorme's *Texas Atlas & Gazetteer:* Page 69 8A. GPS: N30° 06' 677" W97° 16' 132"

This steep canyon, formed by Bee Creek, is seen from Wolf Mountain Trail.

THE HIKE

Start at the trailhead adjacent to the Wolf Mountain Trail parking area. Bear left and initially head east, but you'll soon start meandering as the trail hugs the contour of the hills. With less than a 300-foot rise in elevation, this is not conventional mountain hiking. There are mile markers every half-mile; some of the park signs were made by Eagle Scouts.

Pass the regal creek sign and bear right, heading to the creek. On the left are remnants of a rock wall. A number of short spurs lead to the creek, which runs between steep limestone walls. One of the spurs leads to a rocky outcrop at the edge of an overlook, and then has a sheer 60-foot dropoff, so use caution. Don't expect to see flowing creeks. Park personnel reported in 2007 that the last time the creeks were flowing steadily was in 2005.

Pass a short flat stone retaining wall, about 30 feet long, on the right. This area had been part of the Circle Bar Ranch and the wall was probably part of a fence system.

Pass the bee creek sign and head down to cross the creek. Outcrops and the limestone creek bed make the crossing easy. When the creek is high, Arrowhead Pool is formed and the gurgling of the water running into it is pleasing. Look and listen for canyon wren in the canyon-lined woodlands.

Veer hard left (northeast) after crossing the creek and continue steadily up through the cedar forest. Pass a large live oak tree with short, flat-topped limestone outcrops surrounding it. This makes a great photo op. Look for the large

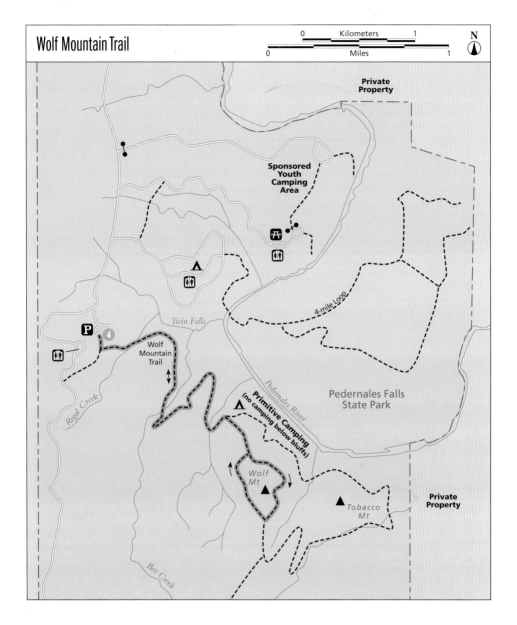

three-pronged bird tracks left by wild turkeys, which are common in the area. Golden-cheeked warblers nest here and can be heard or seen between mid-March and May.

Veer sharply left and head down to Mescal Creek, which crosses the trail. Take a short side trip on the path to the left, along the creek, and head downstream to a small rapid. Return to the trail and bear left, up a steep grade. At the top of the grade is the wolf ridge primitive camp sign. Wild hogs are frequently seen near the campground. Primitive composting toilets are on the left. Since the trail has followed the contours of Wolf Mountain and has been heading up, it is possible to look down and left to see the portion of trail you just came over.

Go up and keep bearing left on the fairly steep grade. Small rocks are strewn about in clearings and under the cedars. As the trail flattens and nears the top, there are good views of the valley and hills. Small flat rocks break the trail surface, making walking a little harder.

Go past clearings on the left: You'll find nice views and a steep slope and dropoff on the right side. At the top of the mountain, the trail flattens and there are sweeping panoramic views of the Pedernales valley.

Veer hard right and continue between the cedars, which now block much of the view. The left edge slopes gently down for about 30 feet and then has a sharp dropoff of 60 feet. To the right of the trail, a limestone ledge resembles a short wall. Make a sweeping right and, depending on the season, pass patches of low-growing mountain pink flowers nestled among the limestone and grass. Near the trail's edge a small circle of rocks, 5 to 7 feet high, some flat, some rectangular, with cedars circling them, makes us marvel at nature's work. The trail meanders a little, with a gravely slope on the left and then a sharp dropoff to valley floor.

At the T, take the left branch and start backtracking, descending from Wolf Mountain. The park has a wheelchair-accessible bird-viewing station, where not only birds but sometimes rattlesnakes and other critters may be seen. There also is a 4-mile Loop trail in the park.

White-tailed deer can be seen along the edges of many trails. Some have become accustomed to hikers, creating good photo ops.

MILES AND DIRECTIONS

Note: This trail has mile markers every 0.5 mile.

0.0 Start at the Wolf Mountain trailhead.

1.0 After following the trail through a sweeping right (south) turn, reach Bee Creek. After crossing the creek, veer sharply left, heading generally north. Bee Creek has a limestone bed and generally is less than 2 feet deep, making crossing easy. Follow the trail as it makes a sweeping bend and heads toward Mescal Creek.

1.8 Reach Mescal Creek. Mescal Creek also has a limestone bed and is generally less than 2 feet deep, making crossing easy. Veer left after crossing the creek. A primitive camping area will be to the north.

2.5 There is a branch where Wolf Mountain Trail continues southeast near Tobacco Mountain or loops around the south side of Wolf Mountain. Turn right, heading west to complete the loop around Wolf Mountain.

2.7 Reach the intersection where the loop began. There is a composting privy here. Veer left (west) and backtrack to the trailhead.

3.8 End the hike at the trailhead.

The mockingbird is the Texas state bird.

Journaling—More Fun on the Trail

If you're not hiking with some specific purpose other than to simply enjoy the outdoors, journaling can be a great way to add a dimension to a family or social hike. A friend of mine had recently given me some instructions on trail observation and how to keep a trail journal. Prior to that I wasn't sure what journaling was. Like the words yodeling and pedaling, it sounds interesting and as though it involves action, but I didn't know what it involved and how this fit in with hiking.

My friend explained that journaling is just keeping a rough set of notes on what you observe on or near the trail. You don't need to be a writer or scientist. The most interesting aspect was the methods of observation. These include closing your eyes and listening, scooping up some dirt to feel, and covering your ears and watching. The idea is to use all of your senses to enhance the experience.

The minimum items needed to start a journal are something to write with and something to write on. Some general rules on how to start the journal: in the upper right-hand corner of the page record the date, time, location, weather, and habitat for each hike. This gives a reference point for future use of the notes. Each hiker records the things that are of interest to him or to her, including drawings. Some folks, like me, have difficulty drawing a stick man; but give it a try, maybe start out with a dandelion.

I decided to try out some of the techniques, which sounded like a great inexpensive family activity. I asked my son Scott, his twelve-year-old son Austin, and Scott's mother, Kay, to accompany me. Scott wasn't sure what I was trying to accomplish. I convinced him that hiking and journaling would give him a chance to slow down and focus on something other than work.

Austin led the way to the trail that paralleled a road. A five-minute limit was set to walk about 75 yards up the trail at a normal pace and 15 minutes to return using our new observation skills. At the end of the 75-yard walk and to our amazement, there wasn't much difference in any of the journals. All had seen trees, bushes, and sky. Austin had seen a couple of worms and a low-flying bee, while Scott noticed a salamander that Kay and I had not recorded. It was now time to start back and make observations.

We stopped every 10–15 yards to listen, watch, touch, smell, and possibly taste. Scott was the only one to taste something, taking some blooms from a honeysuckle bush and showing us they were edible. At each stop we looked straight ahead, then stooped, then stood up, covered our eyes and listened, covered our ears and watched. What we saw and heard became entries in our journals, which included: wind rustling, birds chirping, people, the path, ants, a squirrel climbing a tree, sky with clouds, pine needles and cones, small and large bushes, red flowers, poison ivy, a hole in a tree, a turkey vulture circling in the sky, and pine and hardwood trees.

Things had been felt that were hard, soft, slippery, waxy, coarse, smooth, dry, and wet. Colors noted were green, yellow, brown, black, and white and a rainbow-colored leaf. After discovering something new, we were often surprised at how many times we continued to see it and realized that we must have walked past it many times without seeing it. The return trip almost became a game. The writing stopped being a task and became a fun part of our trip.

Back home, all were excited about the hike. From their enthusiasm, there was no doubt that journaling had added an interesting dimension to the trip. Try it; you could like it.

Three generations of a hiking family rest at a table while reviewing their journal notes.

Berry Springs Park: Muy Grande

This is the only hike in Texas that loops through more than 1,100 pecan trees. It's also the best trail for beginners, families with small children, and persons needing wheelchair access. Follow along Berry Creek to the Mill Pond, where beavers live. There are six interconnecting loops in Berry Springs Park that create 5 miles of trails.

Start: Muy Grande trailhead

Nearest town: Georgetown

Distance: 1.3 miles; interconnecting loops

Approximate hiking time: 1 hour

Difficulty: Easy; the trail is flat, paved and packed gravel

Trail surface: Concrete, gravel

Seasons: Year-round

Other trail users: Dog walkers

Canine compatibility: Leashed dogs permitted

Land status: Williamson County Park; Williamson County Parks & Recreation Department

Fees and permits: No fees or permits required

Schedule: 7:00 a.m. to 10:00 p.m. daily

Maps: The trail map is on the bulletin board at the trailhead. You can also get a map at the Web site, www.wilco.org.

Trail contacts: Williamson County Park, 1801 County Road 152, Georgetown, TX 78626; (512) 260-4283

Finding the trailhead:
From Austin take Interstate 35 north to the Williams Drive exit in Georgetown. Head east, turn left on North Austin Avenue and then right onto Farm Road 971. Turn left onto County Road 152 and continue past the hard right turn in the road. Cross Berry Creek; the park entrance is on the left. The park entrance sign, built from stone, is in the shape of a limestone kiln. Continue into the parking lot. The trailhead adjoins the parking lot. DeLorme's *Texas Atlas & Gazetteer:* Page 69 C11. GPS: N30° 41' 057" W97° 38' 713"

Muy Grande trail in Berry Springs Park passes around the Mill Pond.

THE HIKE

The Muy Grande loop, a concrete, wheelchair-accessible trail in Berry Springs Park, leads both to the right and to the left; take the left branch and more than 1,100 pecan trees, the state tree, come into view. The most striking thing is that the trees, planted in the mid-1920s, are in perfect rows exactly the same distance apart. In the fall, hikers are encouraged to pick up the ripe pecans and take a bag home. Benches are conveniently placed at short intervals along the edge of the trail.

Follow the path to a walk-around circle. Circle to the right: Berry Creek is on the left about 30 yards down and the dam crossing the creek at CR 152 is in sight. The dam, over 160 years old, and the first gristmill in Williamson County, which operated near this site, were built by John Berry. The path changes to packed gravel and is still wheelchair accessible.

Continue straight ahead and, if you're hiking in July and August, the small white flowers of the obedience plant are noticeable along the creek. The plant received its name due to the fact that if one bends the stem, it will take on the new shape. Go past a gravel path that intersects the trail on the right; this is the Mill Pond Loop. Keep going to a boardwalk, actually concrete, which follows the creek for about 350 feet. Midway down the boardwalk on the right side is a limestone dam about 10-feet high that was built in 1846.

Pass a branch in the trail that goes to the semiprimitive camping area. In spring and summer, the raucous cry of "ka, ka, ka, ka, ka, kowp, kowp, kowp, kowp" heard from the treetops can be startling. It is the call of the yellow-billed cuckoo, a medium-size bird with an appetite for tent caterpillars.

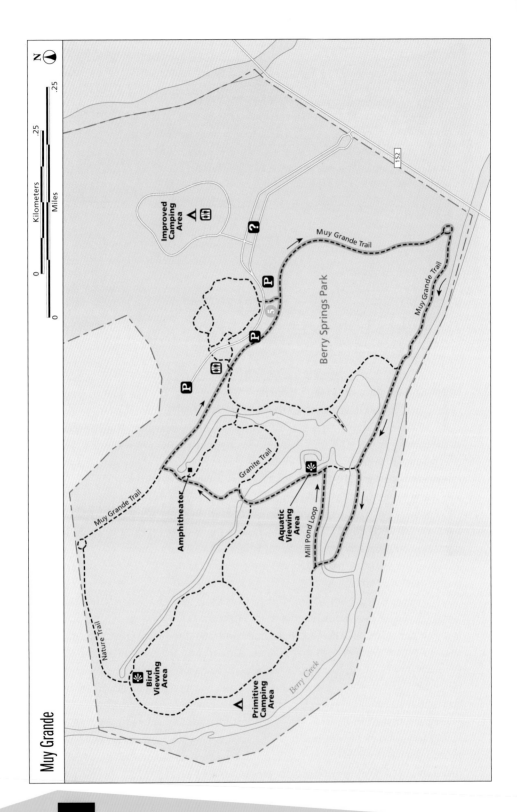

Muy Grande

Improved Camping Area

Berry Springs Park

152

Muy Grande Trail

Muy Grande Trail

Amphitheater

Granite Trail

Aquatic Viewing Area

Mill Pond Loop

Muy Grande Trail

Nature Trail

Bird Viewing Area

Primitive Camping Area

Berry Creek

5

N

Kilometers
0   .25

Miles
0   .25

Follow the path to a concrete bridge that crosses over the 2½-acre spring-fed Mill Pond. The spring water is a constant 68 degrees, and several beavers have homesteaded in the pond. There is a concrete springhead overlook that can be used for catch-and-release fishing.

Continue following the path in a northerly direction until the trail comes to a T at the junction with Pond Loop Trail. Turn right; there is a bench on the left and the pond is on the right. This is about the center of the park and most of the 5 miles of trails are in your line of sight, so any route can be selected. In the spring wildflowers are abundant, including wild geranium and Texas bluebonnets, the state flower.

Travel along the trail past a spur that goes to the amphitheater, and then turn right onto the concrete trail and proceed along a narrow overflow section of Mill Pond. It is only a short distance to a path on the left that goes to the restrooms and a shelter. The Historic Compound, consisting of a 1920s-era house, a barn, and a small granary, is just past the shelter. The trailhead and parking lot are in view.

Berry Springs Park opened in October 2005 and is one of Williamson County's newest parks. John Berry, for whom the park was named, was a pioneer, colonist, gunsmith, blacksmith, and veteran of the War of 1812. He is buried in the small family cemetery located within the park. Audie Murphy, World War II hero and the most decorated soldier in U.S. history, was Berry's great-grandson and also a native of Texas. Small children can easily go on this family-friendly hike and afterwards enjoy the catch-and-release fishing pond.

MILES AND DIRECTIONS

0.0 Start at the Muy Grande trailhead adjacent to the parking area and head left (east).

0.1 Pass a picnic bench on the left. Bear slightly left (east) and then right (south).

0.4 Reach the circle and bear right (west). Berry Creek is on the left (south). Reach concrete boardwalk.

0.7 Boardwalk ends and Muy Grande trail turns to hardpacked gravel. Reach a small concrete bridge crossing the pond overflow.

0.8 Reach a T intersection and follow trail right (east), the pond is on the right.

0.9 Reach another T intersection and turn left (north) toward the amphitheater and Muy Grande Trail.

1.0 Pass a path on the right (east) that leads to the amphitheater. Benches are placed near trail.

1.1 Reach T intersection with Muy Grande. Turn right (east) and continue on Muy Grande.

1.3 End loop at parking lot and trailhead.

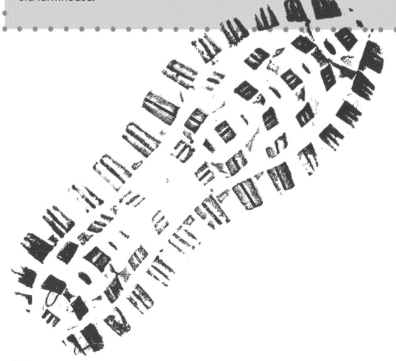

John Berry, Frontiersman

As a young man, John Berry fought in the War of 1812 against Great Britain. He was a native of Kentucky and moved to Texas in 1827. Settling in the area near Mina (now Bastrop) he received several small lots from the Mexican government. (This is the same area in which Stephen F. Austin's Little Colony was established.) Bastrop is the second oldest city in Texas.

Berry lived under Mexican rule until the Texas fight for independence, when he fought with the Texans. His three oldest sons, Joseph, John Bates, and Andrew Jackson, served in the Republic of Texas Army. Joseph was the first casualty in the Mier Expedition. All three were also Texas Rangers. Berry had eighteen children from his three marriages. In 1846, he settled 3 miles northeast of Georgetown, which is now the site of Berry Springs Park.

He built a blacksmith shop, gun shop, and a spring-driven gristmill adjacent to Berry Creek on the spring-fed pond. The mill, the first in Williamson County, was of great importance economically. Customers brought their corn to be ground and no longer had to grind it by hand. The gristmill survived until 1921, when it was washed away by a flood. The original burr stone used to grind the corn is located in an interpretive shelter in Berry Springs Park. The rock dam crossing Berry Creek was built in the mid-1840s and is still standing. John Berry is buried in the cemetery located on the hill behind the old farmhouse.

Balcones Canyonlands National Wildlife Refuge: Cactus Rocks Trail

Texas Hill Country lovers and bird-watchers can combine the Cactus Rocks, Vista Knoll, and Ridgeline Trails to explore the Balcones limestone terraces in the Warbler Vista area of Balcones Canyonlands National Wildlife Refuge. Follow the Vista Knoll Trail down the backbone of a ridge and then back up for panoramic views of the Hill Country and Lake Travis. On the Cactus Rocks Trail, cactus appears to grow out of rocks. Look for "Swiss cheese" limestone rocks riddled with holes. During their fall migration, hundreds of thousands of monarch butterflies flying southward roost here on their journey to the mountains of central Mexico. The winter brings large flocks of robins and cedar waxwings to the refuge.

Start: Cactus Rocks Trail trailhead
Nearest town: Lago Vista
Distance: 3.6 miles out-and-back
Approximate hiking time: 2.5 hours
Difficulty: Moderate due to narrow trails on the edge of a bluff, with ups and downs on rocky trail
Trail surface: Dirt, gravel, limestone outcrop
Seasons: September to June
Other trail users: Bird-watchers from April to June
Canine compatibility: Dogs not permitted
Land status: National wildlife refuge administered by the U.S. Fish and Wildlife Service

Fees and permits: No fees or permits required
Schedule: Sunrise to sunset
Maps: Ask at the refuge office or visit http://friendsofbalcones.org/documents/WV.pdf
Trail contacts: Balcones Canyonlands National Wildlife Refuge, 24518 Farm Road 1431, Box 1, Marble Falls, TX 78654; (512) 339-9432; www.fws.gov/southwest/refuges/texas/balcones
Other: No potable water is available. The only restroom is a portable one by the parking lot for the Cactus Rocks Trail.

Finding the trailhead:
The refuge is 30 minutes from Austin. From the capital, head north on U.S. Highway 183 to Cedar Park, about 14 miles. Turn left (west) onto FM 1431 and continue through Jamestown and Lago Vista. Turn right onto Farm Road 1174 and head north for about 5 miles. On the west side of Lago Vista look for the balcones canyonlands national wildlife refuge sign on the right, and turn onto the gravel road. Drive downhill on the gravel road 0.75 mile to the Cactus

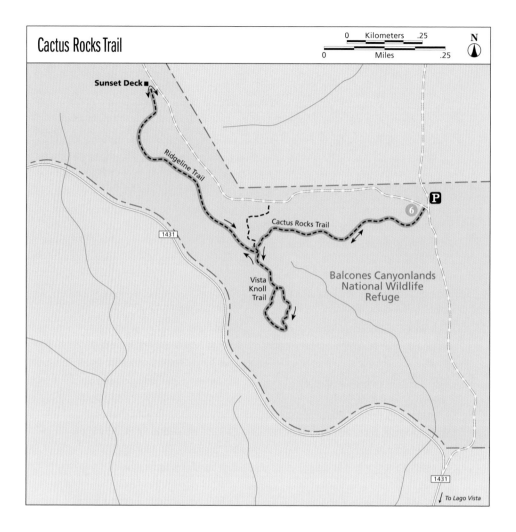

Kilometers
0   .25

Miles
0   .25

N

Sunset Deck ■

Ridgeline Trail

Cactus Rocks Trail

1431

P

6

Vista
Knoll
Trail

Balcones Canyonlands
National Wildlife
Refuge

1431

To Lago Vista

Rocks parking area, next to the interpretive trail guide display. The trailhead is south of the park road and across from the parking lot. DeLorme's *Texas Atlas & Gazetteer:* Page 69 E9. GPS: N30° 30' 335" W97° 58' 784"

THE HIKE

Pick up an interpretive trail brochure at the bulletin board located at the trailhead. Hike into the cedar woods, walking on bark mulch put there by Boy Scout Troop 77 from Lago Vista. The group also made many of the trail signs. The Central Texas Trail Tamers and other volunteers furnished much of the labor to build the trails.

Interpretive marker 1 is about 100 feet down the trail and on the right. These markers are unique in that they are made from limestone, with the face flattened and painted with the marker number and a picture of the golden-cheeked warbler. The Balcones Canyonlands National Wildlife Refuge, with more than 80,000 acres, was established to preserve habitat for the endangered warbler, which nests only in central Texas, and also to help conserve the natural diversity of wildlife.

Head west and follow the contour of the ridge, where the rimrock outcrops can be seen. The cedars and a few oak trees form an overhead arch giving welcome shade from the sun.

Go down and up the sides of some dry gullies and pass prickly pear cactus growing from boulders and limestone outcroppings. The trail was named for the cactus that grow from the scant soil collected in the cracks and depressions in the rocks. Another interesting feature of the rocks is their "Swiss cheese" appearance— some of them are riddled with holes.

In the spring, butterflies gather nectar from the prickly pear cactus,
the state plant of Texas.

> *Balcones Canyonlands National Wildlife Refuge has identified more than 525 plant species within its boundaries. Included in these is the newly discovered Texabama croton, an 8- to 10-foot tall shrub with white flowers in February and March. At least a third of all the threatened and endangered species in Texas live or move through the refuge.*

At the end of the Cactus Rocks Trail, veer left (east, then south) onto the Vista Knoll Trail. Descend down the backbone of the ridge to some limestone *balcones* that afford views of Lake Travis and the surrounding countryside. When Spanish explorers first saw the hills northwest of what is now Austin, they named the land *balcones* for the terraced and sometimes almost stairlike rock formations that adjoin lush canyons. These limestone hills and spring-fed canyons make up most of the Balcones Canyonlands National Wildlife Refuge. The Great Plains and Gulf Coast geographic regions join at Balcones Canyonlands. Add to this the unusual limestone geology of the Edwards Plateau and you've got the Hill Country, an area unique to central Texas.

The trail gets rockier and has less tree cover as it loops around much of a small hill. Limestone outcroppings sometimes cover the path, making walking difficult. Openings in the cedar and oak woods offer panoramic views from several locations.

Complete the loop and connect with Ridgeline Trail, which leads left (northwest) to the Sunset Deck. The covered deck offers a view of Lake Travis while providing the opportunity to hear or see the black-crested titmouse, Carolina chickadee, and scrub jay, which are Hill Country specialties.

While backtracking to the intersection with the Vista Knoll Trail, watch for fox squirrels, the most common squirrel in Texas. It is named for its gray- and red-colored fur that resembles the pelt of a gray fox. Look for their nests about 30 feet up at a major fork in a tree. They are usually active early in the morning and late in the afternoon. Those maple, oak, or pine trees you admire so much in the fall may have grown from the leftovers of a squirrel's unfinished meal. Squirrels find only a portion of the nuts they bury and are important in planting many species of nut trees.

After reaching Vista Knoll it is only a short distance to the intersection with Cactus Rocks Trail and your return to the parking area.

0.0   Start at the Cactus Rocks Trailhead, adjacent to the parking area, and head west on Cactus Rocks Trail toward the junction with the Vista Knoll Trail.

0.6   Reach the T intersection with Vista Knoll Trail. Take the left branch, heading south-southeast. Follow the trail heading south and stay left, following the loop clockwise and back to where it links with Ridgeline Trail.

1.5   Ridgeline Trail joins Vista Knoll. Turn left (northwest) and follow Ridgeline Trail to the Sunset Deck observation shelter.

2.3   Reach the Sunset Deck observation shelter at the end of the Ridgeline Trail. Backtrack to the intersection with the Vista Knoll Trail.

3.0   Ridgeline Trail intersects Vista Knoll Trail. Turn left onto Vista Knoll, heading north for a short distance to where Cactus Rocks Trail intersects on the right (east). Turn right on Cactus Rocks and backtrack to the trailhead and parking area.

3.6   End the hike at the trailhead at the Cactus Rocks parking area.

Local Information

For information on Lago Vista, visit the Lago Vista Chamber of Commerce Web site at www.lagovista.org.

Swiss Cheese Rocks

In the Hill Country it is not unusual to see rocks riddled with holes similar to those in Swiss cheese. The rocks range from fist-size to boulders, usually are found in small groups, and are composed of limestone. Two parks in the area, Warbler Vista in the Balcones Canyonlands National Wildlife Refuge and the Friedrich Natural Area in San Antonio, have excellent examples along the trail.

The limestone is 80 to 120 million years old and is the bedrock in many areas. It started out as mud in shallow lagoons, where worms and mollusks worked their way through creating numerous tunnels. The mud sediment eventually hardened into limestone, leaving the holes filled with softer material. This material eroded out of the rock and the Swiss-cheese holes remained. Sometimes dirt and other material fill the holes, and plants, including cactus, take root, giving the appearance of growing from the rock.

Emma Long Metropolitan Park: Turkey Creek Trail

Turkey Creek is the hike for creek lovers and dog lovers. Dogs love to splash in the water as the creek is crossed no less than fourteen times. A number of clear pools along the banks offer more splashing opportunities. A variety of vegetation, including cedar, cedar elm, live oak, and mountain laurel, lines the creek bed. Follow a modest ascent from the creek, leaving the valley, to the top of the bluff, and break into the open sky at the canyon rim. Look down on the bluff walls and across the top for panoramic views.

Start: Turkey Creek trailhead
Nearest town: Austin
Distance: 2.6-mile lollipop
Approximate hiking time: 1.5 hours
Difficulty: Moderate due to a 250-foot gain in elevation up a steep hill, and some rocky terrain
Trail surface: Dirt path
Seasons: September to July
Other trail users: Dog walkers
Canine compatibility: Dogs permitted
Land status: City park; Austin Parks and Recreation Department

Fees and permits: No fees or permits required
Schedule: 7:00 a.m. to 10:00 p.m. daily
Maps: Maps are available at the park office and on the Web site ci.austin.tx.us/parks/parkdirectory .htm.
Trail contacts: Austin Parks and Recreation Department, 1600 City Park Road, Austin, TX 78730; (512) 346-3807; (512) 974-6700
Other: There is no restroom or water available at the trailhead.

Finding the trailhead:
From central Austin, take Farm Road 2222 west, past Loop 360. Turn left onto City Park Road and continue south to the emma long park entrance sign. The parking area for the trail is on the right-hand side of the road 2 miles from the entrance. The sign in the parking lot identifies the trail as nature trail. The trailhead is adjacent to the parking lot and has a signboard with a map and trail information. DeLorme's *Texas Atlas & Gazetteer:* Page 93 C5. GPS: N30° 20' 008" W97° 50' 400"

This is one of only a few trails in the Austin area that allow dogs to be off-leash. The upside is that the dogs, and sometimes their owners, enjoy uninhibited splashing in the creek; the downside is that the opportunity to see wildlife, other than birds, is rare.

Several signs warn hikers to stay on the marked trail, since the area furnishes habitat for the endangered golden-cheeked warbler.

As you get under way, follow the trail for a short distance parallel to City Park Road, and then cross over concrete stepping stones to the west side of Turkey Creek. The creek is normally less than a foot deep, but after a rain the water can rise above the stones. Plan to get wet crossing the creek if there has been more than 2 to 3 inches of rain in the day(s) prior to hiking. This is the first of many creek crossings, shifting back and forth from the west side to the east side. Cedar trees furnish good cover and provide a cooling effect, especially welcome in the summer.

After the first creek crossing, the trail heads generally north toward the Fern Wall. As the trail hugs the bank, there are opportunities for great photos looking up and downstream, with much of the creek bed made up of exposed limestone typical of the geology of the Balcones Escarpment. There is a large flat limestone outcrop in the creek bed just after the branch that begins the loop, which makes crossing the creek easier.

Grottos, overhanging limestone rock formations along creeks and rivers, are covered with plant life and can be seen on several trails in the Hill Country.

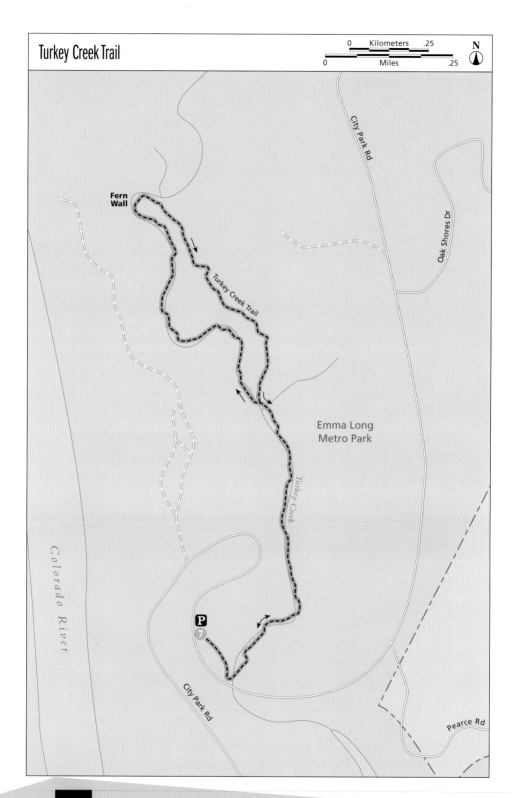

Turkey Creek Trail

Fern
Wall

Turkey Creek Trail

City Park Rd

Oak Shores Dr

Emma Long
Metro Park

Turkey Creek

Colorado River

City Park Rd

Pearce Rd

P
7

0 ___ Kilometers ___ .25
0 ___ Miles ___ .25

N

At the fork, take the left branch; this keeps the mile markers in sequence. The trail closely follows the creek for about 1.25 miles, until you reach the Fern Wall. This wall, 40- to 50-feet high and alive with maidenhair ferns in the spring, is one of the limestone bluffs that border parts of the creek.

After passing the Fern Wall, the trail heads south. Along the creek bank the cedars are joined by a few live oak, tall cedar elms, and sycamore trees. There have been ten creek crossings by the time the 1.5-mile marker is reached.

The trail ascends about 250 feet and wanders away from Turkey Creek. The path is steep, with rocks and outcrops of limestone forming steps. Along the trail are good examples of "Swiss cheese" rocks; these can range from fist-size to boulders. The holes were formed in the limestone by worms making tunnels millions of years ago.

The top is reached near the 1.5-mile marker, where the terrain flattens and becomes more open. In the spring bluebonnets, the state flower, grow in the grassy openings between the cedars. Several paths lead to overlooks where great views of the creek and valley can be seen. Be careful when approaching the edge of the bluff since there are 40- to 50-foot dropoffs. On the way down from the summit there are more limestone steps, some dropping 5 feet down to the next step.

Coming up the hill to the top and starting the descent down are the most strenuous parts of the hike. Going down, the path squirms though stands of cedars and reaches the creek. When the branch connecting the loop is reached, backtrack to the trailhead.

Emma Long Metro Park is one of many parks that the Civilian Conservation Corps (CCC) helped build. The CCC was established by President Franklin D. Roosevelt as a work relief program for young men to combat unemployment during the Great Depression. The park was completed in 1939 through the efforts of 200 young men.

The Capitol Area Boy Scouts, along with other groups, built and maintain the trail.

Emma Long Metropolitan Park was originally known as City Park. In 1984 it was renamed to honor Emma Long, the first woman to serve on the Austin City Council.

🌿 Green Tip:
On the trail eat grains and veggies instead of meat, which has a higher energy cost.

0.0   Start at the Turkey Creek trailhead adjacent to the parking area. Trail markers are placed at quarter-mile intervals.

0.75   Reach the branch that begins the loop. Take the left leg, along the creek edge, to walk the loop clockwise. This also keeps the mile-markers in sequence.

1.0   Reach a mile marker. Turkey Creek will have been crossed eight times at this point.

1.5   A path near the top of the bluff leads to an overlook of the creek and valley.

2.0   Reach the branch connecting the loop. Continue south on the trail and backtrack to the trailhead.

2.6   End at the trailhead and parking lot.

"I Came Storming In . . . "

In Austin, Texas, in 1948, a woman could vote, but could not serve on a jury, enter into a contract, or bring suit in her own name (among other things). Bucking the rules and "storming in," Emma Long was the first woman elected to the Austin City Council. This also made her the first woman elected to any major city council in the state.

Almost immediately after being elected, she reactivated the Parks and Recreation Board. She introduced civil rights ordinances and scored many firsts for women in politics during her sixteen years on the council. Cactus Pryor was quoted in the *Austin American-Statesman* on April 13, 1969, with this praise: "To my knowledge she has always been completely honest, and honesty means frankness which can sometimes be painful, depending on where you are standing. But you always knew exactly where Councilwoman Long stood . . . and sometimes it was on your neck."

In 1984 Carol Keeton Rylander, mayor of Austin from 1977 to 1983, proposed that City Park be renamed Emma Long Metropolitan Park to honor this remarkable woman.

"I came storming in," said Emma Long about her birth in 1912 during a Texas Panhandle snowstorm. "The doctor had to come out in a sled to deliver me." Fortunately for the city of Austin, storming she stayed.

St. Edwards Park: Hill and Creek Trails

St. Edwards Park offers a split personality—a high limestone bluff and flat lowlands separated by Bull Creek. Cross over slightly submerged rocks to the south side of Bull Creek and the Hill Trail. A steep section over limestone outcrops leads to the top, where a single-track trail clings to the edge of the bluff. There are impressive vistas of the countryside though clearings in the cedars. The next section is more strenuous, with rocky, steep inclines and declines. Head down and cross the creek to the Creek Trail, with its flat and open trails.

Start: Trailhead adjacent to the parking lot
Nearest town: Austin
Distance: 1.2-mile lollipop
Approximate hiking time: 1.5 hours
Difficulty: Moderate due to steep inclines and declines over rocky terrain on the Hill Trail
Trail surface: Dirt, stones, limestone outcrops
Seasons: October to June
Other trail users: Dog walkers
Canine compatibility: Leashed dogs permitted. Dogs are not recommended on the Hill Trail due to the rocky terrain and the single-track trail on the edge of the bluff.
Land status: City park; Austin Parks and Recreation Department
Fees and permits: No fees or permits required
Schedule: 5:00 a.m. to 10:00 p.m.
Maps: Visit www.ci.austin.tx.us/parks/traildirectory.htm for maps.
Trail contacts: Austin Parks and Recreation Department, 7301 Spicewood Springs Road, Austin, TX 78767; (512) 346-3807
Other: There is no potable water in the park. No restroom facilities are available.

Finding the trailhead:
From U.S. Highway 183 in Austin, take the Capitol of Texas Highway south to Spicewood Springs Road. Turn right (west) and go about 5 miles. Pass Bridge 5 and go 0.25 mile. The park entrance is on the left at 7301 Spicewood Springs Road. There are two trailhead posts. Start at the one to the left. DeLorme's *Texas Atlas & Gazetteer:* Page 92 A7. GPS: N30° 24' 390' W97° 47' 413"

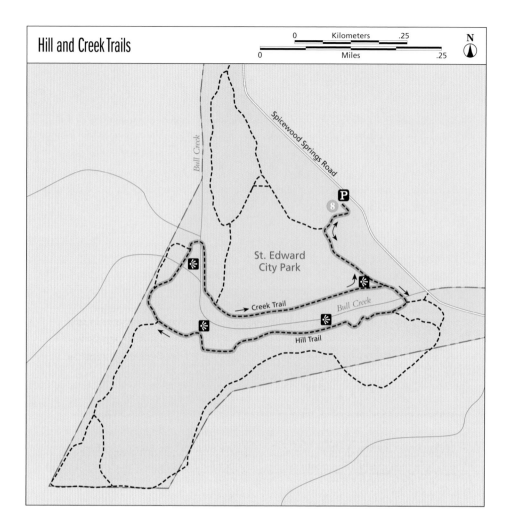

THE HIKE

G rassy areas with cedars and prickly pear cactus are interspersed on each side of the trail. Follow a gentle slope down, heading to Bull Creek. There is a narrow rock and concrete dam that some folks use to get across, but there is no trail to follow at the other side of the dam. Rocks have been appropriately placed in the water to aid in crossing. Depending on the amount of recent rainfall, getting to the other side can be slippery and wet. The creek is shallow, so wading across is always an option.

This is an ecologically sensitive area. Bull Creek is part of the Bull Creek watershed. A city park sign on the opposite side of the creek informs visitors that this section of St. Edwards Park operates as part of the Balcones Canyonlands Conservation Program and has slightly different rules.

Now on the Hill Trail, climb about 50 feet up and over limestone outcroppings to where the trail levels. There are sections of single-track that hug the edge of the bluff and have sheer dropoffs to the creek bed. This requires caution, since small rocks and sometimes tree roots are in the path. Bear left and go up some steep limestone "steps" that lead to a flat area near the top of the bluff. There are a few rocks that are large enough to sit on and take a rest after the climb.

Several trails enter this area, but continue to the right, heading west along the edge of the bluff. Clearings between the cedar and oak trees allow panoramic views of the creek lowlands and northeast Austin. Go over some rocky outcrops and the rimrock to reach the top of the bluff. The stillness, silence, and serenity here make it difficult to believe this is in Austin.

Take the path to the right and head slightly down to a boundary fence, where the trail makes a hard right. Getting to the top and getting down are the most strenuous parts of the hike. Go steeply downhill for about 75 feet over solid limestone outcrops, some requiring a step down of 3 feet.

The path goes up and down, still along the fence, and then through several dry-wash gullies. At points the path is single-track with the fence on one side and heavy woodlands on the other. The trail widens, still in the cedar and oak woods, and heads away from the fence toward the creek. The creek comes into view and is wide, with gravel, sandbars, and a few trees, making an ideal watering hole for deer.

Some of the trails running along creeks are single track, with rocks and other obstructions, challenging the hiker.

Many trails follow creeks that have eroded limestone walls.
These offer a shady spot to rest or have a picnic.

The path along the north side of the creek leads to and dead-ends at limestone bluffs bordering it. This out-and-back path is the only place in the park where the bluffs can be viewed. After a wet season, small waterfalls trickle down the face of the bluffs. The path is narrow and overgrown, and it appears that not many folks get here.

Backtrack to the point where you turned onto this path. Scattered rocks have been placed in the water to help crossing to the Creek Trail. Once on Creek Trail the canopy is open, with cedars, a few cactus, and tall grass bordering the path. Go past numerous branches, generally staying right. Continue following the trail back to the parking area.

This park has a proliferation of unmarked paths. Fortunately getting lost is not a major problem if you use the bluff, Bull Creek, and Spicewood Springs Road as reference points. Although this hike is short, it is invigorating and scenic.

MILES AND DIRECTIONS

0.0   Start at the Creek Trail trailhead adjacent to the parking area. Creek Trail leads to junction with Hill Trail across Bull Creek.

0.1   After leaving the trailhead, quickly reach a Y. (It is actually less than 100 yards.) Take the left (west) leg and continue left past another branch. Many of these paths have been made by hikers and wander through the park. Follow Keith's Route on map.

0.2   Reach Bull Creek. Spicewood Springs Road can be seen about 50 yards to the left (east). Cross Bull Creek to the trailhead for Hill Trail. Continue across a trail that passes on the left and right and start up the hill. Limestone steps lead to a T. Take the right leg and head west, following Bull Creek.

0.3   Near the top of the bluff, there is a flat open area where three other trails enter. Continue right (west) along the edge of the bluff and overlooking the creek.

0.6   Reach the top of the bluff, which overlooks Bull Creek to the north. Other trails enter the area on the left, but continue bearing right, close to the edge of the bluff.

0.7   Reach Keith's Overlook (named for yours truly) for a clear view of Bull Creek plains. Start steep descent down to creek.

0.8   After descent, reach east side of Bull Creek. At this point the creek flows north and south. Turn right on a path that heads south, go about 30 yards to where it dead-ends at a limestone bluff. This is the only place where the bluffs can be reached. Backtrack to Hill Trail and ford Bull Creek to the Creek Trail.

0.9   Bear left (east) on Creek Trail. Bull Creek is on the right.

1.1   Make a hard left (north) turn and backtrack to the trailhead.

1.2   End the hike back at the trailhead and parking area.

James Stephen Hogg, born in 1851 near Rusk, was the first native Texan to be elected governor. He was one of the original investors in Texaco. His daughter, Ima Hogg, was a major benefactor to the Houston Symphony, state parks, and many buildings and cultural events.

Southeast Metropolitan Park: Primitive Trail

Hiking nearly 3 miles up, down, and around the backbone of a ridge, with forest, cactus, and undergrowth reaching to the trail's edge, makes this feel like the wilderness. Two ponds offer resting points on their fishing piers. Downtown Austin can be seen from one of the overlooks. There are opportunities for wildlife viewing and bird-watching, and spring offers abundant displays of blooming prickly pear cactus and wildflowers. This is acknowledged as the best hike in eastern Travis County.

Start: Primitive Trail trailhead

Nearest town: Austin

Distance: 2.6-mile loop

Approximate hiking time: 1.75 hours

Difficulty: Moderate due to some steep inclines up the ridge

Trail surface: Gravel, dirt path

Seasons: Year-round

Other trail users: Joggers, dog walkers

Canine compatibility: Leashed dogs permitted

Land status: Travis County Park

Fees and permits: No fees or permits required

Schedule: Open 8:00 a.m. to 9:00 p.m. May 1 to September 15. Opens at 9:00 a.m. rest of year. Closes at 7:30 p.m. fall and spring, at 6:00 p.m. November 1 to March 1.

Maps: A large map is mounted on the board at the trailhead.

Trail contacts: Travis County Park Department, 1010 Lavaca Street, Austin, TX 78701; (512) 854-7275

Finding the trailhead:
From Austin take Interstate 35 to Highway 71 and head east. Go past Austin-Bergstrom International Airport, and look for the park on the left about 2 miles beyond. There are signs along Highway 71. After entering the park, veer to the right and follow the signs indicating a hiking trail all the way back to the parking area next to the trailhead. DeLorme's *Texas Atlas & Gazetteer:* Page 69 G11. GPS: N30° 11' 658" W97° 36' 570"

A male great egret in breeding plumage. Breeding takes place in March and April.

THE HIKE

Start on the Primitive Trail, reputed to be the best in the southeast Austin area. No maps are available, but there is a large map board at the trailhead. Trail markers are numbered 1 through 60. Head northeast, following along the backbone of the ridge and quickly come to trail marker 1, with a sign pointing to the left stating WILDLIFE VIEWING BLIND.

Continue straight, around cedars, oaks, and prickly pear cactus, the state plant. A wide set of wooden stairs leads to a scenic overlook that on a clear day includes a glimpse of downtown Austin.

Almost immediately beyond the overlook, you'll come to the intersection of the east and west branches of the Primitive Trail. Take the left branch, going west. A gully on the right is full of downed cedars. Butterflies, dragonflies, and moths are numerous. Cross several dry streambeds and gullies; many have bridges. The trail meanders around, going up and down the steep ridgeline, and then heads north. The area is heavily wooded and a variety of shrubs grow to the edge of the trail.

After a short distance, a path on the left leads to an unnamed small pond. A pier reaches over the water, and catch-and-release fishing is allowed. Near the pond the route splits: The left branch is a service road that loops back to the trailhead. Keep to the right, heading east to stay on the trail. The pleasant chatter of birds hidden in the woods breaks the otherwise silent hike. Another pond comes into view on the right; it has a covered fishing pier.

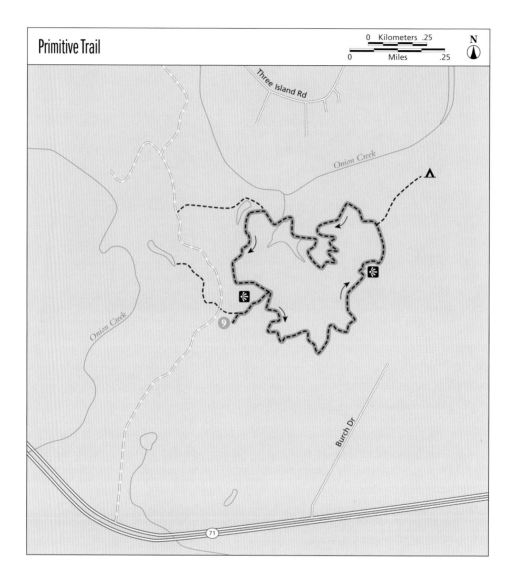

Cross a narrow section of the pond that has concrete embankments on each side. Some American Beauty bushes have large quantities of small blue berries, a favorite food of wildlife, during the summer. The soft bank around the ponds is a good place to look for animal and bird tracks.

Start bearing away from the pond at marker 18 and continue north through a canyon and back up the ridge. This is the steepest section of the hike and is great cardiovascular exercise. As the hike goes through the cedar and oak forest, there is good canopy cover providing welcome shade. Come to an overgrown path that intersects the trail on the left and leads to a primitive camping area. Some of the trail is single-track.

Continue south on the loop and reach another overlook high on the ridge, offering scenic views of the wooded valley below. Steps have been strategically placed to aid in ascending and descending the ridge. Step over some humps spanning the width of the trail. These are not speed bumps meant to slow down joggers—they are water bars, pieces of lumber generally covered by gravel that help channel water off the trail and reduce erosion.

The trail heads down and then follows the contours of the ridge to an intersection on the left (west). Take the left fork to the WILDLIFE VIEWING BLIND sign and then turn right (north). This is a short out-and-back path that leads to the edge of a pond and the blind. Wildlife, especially birds, can be observed here. Onion Creek is to the southwest, but not visible.

Return to the Primitive Trail and turn right to go the short distance back to the trailhead. This hike, except for the trail markers and bridges, gives the feeling of being in the backcountry. Southeast Metropolitan Park also contains a 2-mile concrete, wheelchair-accessible, multiuse trail.

MILES AND DIRECTIONS

0.0 Start at the Primitive Trail trailhead adjacent to the parking area.

0.1 Reach a shelter. Go down the stairs and make a hard right turn.

0.2 Go down six steps to a wooden bridge crossing a gully about 25 feet wide.

0.3 Pass trail marker 8. Continue following the trail to the right.

0.5 Pass a covered fishing pier at the edge of a pond. Catch-and-release fishing is allowed.

0.6 A pond is on the right. Cross a concrete embankment to get to the trail. This walkway can be flooded after a heavy rain.

1.0 Bear left at trail marker 25, then cross a bridge over a gully.

1.4 Pass the group camping sign, near trail marker 35.

1.7 A bridge crosses a narrow gully.

2.0 Pass trail marker 48 and immediately go down three steps to cross another bridge. These bridges are an aid due to the rough terrain. Follow the trail to the right after crossing the bridge.

2.2 Cross a bridge that is identified as number 5. This bridge goes over a dry creek bed.

2.5 Pass the sign for the WILDLIFE VIEWING BLIND.

2.6 End the hike at the trailhead and parking lot.

They Are Not Speed Bumps

If they're on the trail, you'll notice them. I'm talking about those humps and sometimes exposed timbers or rocks crossing some of the sloping or hilly trails. These are water bars, not speed bumps meant to slow down joggers or create obstacles for bikers. Their purpose is to help minimize erosion by channeling water away from the trail. Water that is properly directed can be an asset by playing a role in vegetation growth and natural succession. Uncontrolled erosion can affect the entire area's hydrology.

Water bars can be seen in a wide variety of shapes and materials, depending on the terrain. Most on hiking trails are either exposed wood, wood covered by gravel, or rock. These erosion control devices are considered Band-Aids by "purist" trail designers. They feel their use is required on a poorly designed trail or a trail that is forced into a grade that is too steep due to the terrain. Most new trails do not require water bars, because the design criteria and trail-builders are using more advanced techniques. This means that both art, for the trail aesthetics, and science, to make the trail more stable and accessible, are used in these new trails.

At times it may not seem like it, but trail-builders attempt to make the water bars as user-friendly as possible. One way is to keep the height at a reasonable level for the hiker, versus the optimum level to channel the water. Sometimes water bars appear as stairs, particularly on very steep grades. Hiker safety is also an issue.

Another type of erosion control is the "rolling dip." This method uses earth or other materials found around the trail to build up and support the trail. To create "bumps," if you will, to direct water runoff. A rolling dip has the advantage that on a multi-use trail, bikers can easily navigate it and hikers are less likely to twist their ankles. If the erosion control method is not user-friendly, hikers tend to go around it. This causes two problems: 1) the trail is widened, possibly treading over eco-sensitive areas, and 2) a new runway for water can be created, causing even more erosion.

Water bars may be seen on many trails, including the following: Pecan Flats (hike 1); Primitive Trail (hike 9); Lost Pines (hike 14); Red/Green (hike 17); and Main Loop (hike 29). Some park managers, such as at the Schreiner Natural Area in San Antonio, offer courses for their volunteers, on how to construct and maintain water bars.

Here, I had always thought that logs were simply laid across a trail at an angle to lead water away from the path. So much for my simple bliss.

Logs with interesting fungus growth can be found along many of the trails in forested areas.

McKinney Roughs Nature Park: Riverside Trails

This route combines the best of the 17 miles of McKinney Rough Nature Park's crisscrossed collection of loops and out-and-back trails into one spectacular 2.5-mile hike. Start from the flat ridgetop, then head down to the Colorado River and back, getting sweeping views of rolling box canyons, steep ravines, juniper and oak forests, wildflower meadows, pocket prairies, lazy river bends, and the river itself. Pass through four Texas eco-regions; post oak savanna, blackland prairie, east Texas piney woods, and central Texas plateau. The trails range from easy to difficult as they snake up and down wooded hillsides and through the river bottomland.

Start: Trailhead behind the Environmental Learning Center

Nearest town: Austin

Distance: 2.5-mile loop

Approximate hiking time: 1.75 hours

Difficulty: Easy to moderate due to sandy and sometimes muddy soil by the river. Some single-track with minor grades

Trail surface: Dirt, rocky hardpan, packed gravel, and sand

Seasons: Year-round

Other trail users: Equestrians, dog walkers

Canine compatibility: Leashed dogs permitted

Land status: Lower Colorado River Authority park

Fees and permits: $3 for adults, $1 seniors; no charge for children 13 and under

Schedule: 8:00 a.m. to 5:00 p.m.; day use only

Maps: Trail maps are available in the park office, and also on the Web site www.lcra.org/library/media/public/docs/community_mck_roughs_trailmap.pdf.

Trail contacts: McKinney Roughs Nature Park, 1884 Highway 71 West, Cedar Creek, TX 78612; (512) 303-5073

Other: Always check in at the visitor center before hiking, pay your fee, and get a trail map and information. Fee includes the opportunity to borrow one of the nature packs offered at the park: Birding Pack with binoculars and guidebook; Plant Pack with magnifying glass and explanation of what plants to look for; Kid Pack with bug containers and children's books describing plants, birds, and insects found at the park.

Finding the trailhead:
From Austin, head east on Highway 71 past Austin-Bergstom International Airport. Proceed for about 13 miles beyond the airport, and look for the park's distinctive rock-wall entrance with a windmill on the left (north). Hikers should check in at the Lower Colorado River Authority (LCRA) office near the main parking area. The main hiking trailhead is behind the Environmental Learning Center, adjacent to the main parking lot. DeLorme's *Texas Atlas & Gazetteer:* Page 69 G11. GPS: N30° 11' 653" W97° 36' 572"

THE HIKE

To begin, head north toward the Colorado River, about a mile away. As the trail descends into the bottomlands of the river, the higher plateau rises on each side. The trail between the ridges heads generally east and then bends left, heading north. Most of the tree cover consists of a combination of cedar and oak. Clumps of low-growing cactus grow under the cedars. Several trails intercept the Riverside Trail, including Fox Tail, Pine Ridge, Valley View, Bobcat Ridge, Bluestem, and Cypress. A number of these are short connector trails to the major loop trails. This gives hikers the capability to shorten, lengthen, and alter the route on the go. All the trails have signs that point back to the headquarters. This is handy if the hike has been altered, as it keeps you oriented as to whether you're coming or going.

An overlook view shows the Colorado River in the valley from a trail in McKinney Roughs Nature Park, just outside of Austin.

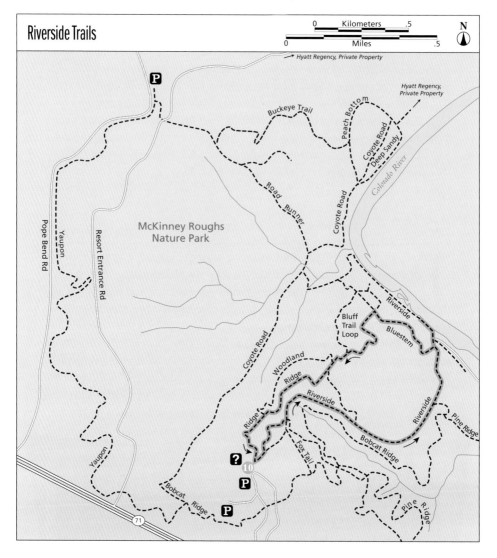

The trail narrows, some sections being single-track, and as it gets closer to the river, the pockets of wildflowers that were seen on the bluff disappear. The ground is covered with various grasses and an abundance of poison ivy. In summer, the area by the river can be 10 to 15 degrees cooler, giving a welcome respite from the heat. If it has rained recently, clay-based mud makes up parts of the trail near the river. Some folks claim that if you spray your boots with nonstick cooking spray, the mud doesn't stick.

Riverside Trail is shared with equestrians, and the hooves of their horses cut up the soil and create mud. This can be avoided by hiking Ridge, Woodland, Cypress, Pine Ridge, Valley View, and Bluff Loop trails, which total more than 5 miles. These are hiking only and have low bars at the trailhead, blocking horses.

Upon reaching the river continue for about a quarter-mile northwest on a short out-and-back path to see the various types of vegetation. The river's edge is a good place to look for animal signs, especially their tracks. This can be fun and adds another dimension to the hike.

Backtrack to the junction with the Bluestem Trail, turn right (northwest) onto Bluestem, and proceed to where the Bluff Trail Loop crosses it. There are some zigs and zags with some steep sections as the short connector trail heads back up to the ridgeline.

Turn left (southwest) onto the east section of Bluff Trail Loop. This section closely follows the contour of the bluff as it winds through the landscape. There are several lookout points where you can view the Colorado River, and it is possible to see segments of the previously hiked Riverside Trail.

Legend has it that in the 1800s, the steep ravines and thick woods of McKinney Roughs provided refuge for frontier outlaws.

Continue around the loop to where Ridge Trails runs into it. Turn left (southwest) onto Ridge Trail, which has a surface of packed gravel making it wheelchair accessible. Interpretive signs placed by local area Boy Scout troops describe the various flowers seen in the open meadows. Benches and a few picnic tables are placed near the signs, making a space to rest and contemplate. There are several sweeping overlooks into a box canyon below. This is not a conventional box canyon with three sides bordered by high walls; instead it is a rolling canyon about 90 feet deep, with no obvious entrance. This is typical of other box canyons in the area.

In May it's possible to see flocks, called "waves," of warblers. The yellow-rumped warbler, with a distinctive lemon-yellow patch above its tail and on its side, is one of the most common. Look high in the trees or listen for a high-pitched "wee-o wee-o" sung by the males. Take some binoculars and a field guide to birds and enjoy the show.

Pass both junctions with the Woodland connector loop, then bend left to get back to the trailhead. Greater roadrunners (beep! beep!), running along with their tails pointing upward just like in the cartoon, are resident birds and are sometimes seen close to the Environmental Center. Cowboys called the roadrunner the "chaparral cock."

McKinney Roughs Nature Park contains the most extensive collection of varied hiking trails in central Texas, so if you've got the time and the inclination, you can sample more.

In pioneer times in McKinney Roughs Nature Park, people who had died were sometimes buried in hollow oak trees. Relatives cut the top off the tree, placed the deceased in the hollow, and covered them with rocks. This was done when the soil was too hard to dig a grave.

Indians made tea from yaupon leaves. The yaupon trees like to grow under oaks and are currently considered an invasive species.

MILES AND DIRECTIONS

0.0   Start at the Riverside Trail trailhead behind the Environmental Learning Center building.

0.1   On the right (north), Fox Tail and Pine Ridge Trails intersect and end at Riverside Trail. Continue on Riverside Trail as it bends left.

0.3   On the left (north), Valley View Trail intersects and ends at Riverside Trail. Continue forward (southeast) and then bear left on Riverside Trail.

0.7   On the right (east), Bobcat Ridge Trail intersects and ends at Riverside Trail. Continue by bearing left (north) on Riverside Trail.

0.9   On the left (west), Bluestem Trail intersects and ends at Riverside Trail, and on the right (east), Cypress Trail intersects and ends at Riverside Trail. Bend left (north) and quickly bear left (northeast) on Riverside Trail. The Colorado River is in view on the right. Hike along the Colorado River for about 0.25 mile, and then backtrack to the intersection with Bluestem Trail.

1.4   Turn right at the intersection with Bluestem Trail and continue northwest to the T intersection with Bluff Trail Loop.

1.5   Take the left fork onto the Bluff Trail Loop, heading south. Cross some dry streambeds.

1.8   Pass the western leg of the Bluff Trail Loop on the right. Continue to where the Ridge Trail intersects with the Bluff Trail Loop. Continue on the Ridge Trail, which is packed gravel and wheelchair accessible. Some outcroppings of limestone are on the trail. On the right, the north section of Woodland Trail intersects and ends at Ridge Trail.

2.2   On the right, the south section of Woodland Trail intersects and ends at Ridge Trail. Continue heading south on Ridge Trail.

2.5   End the hike back at the trailhead by the Environmental Learning Center.

McKinney Roughs Nature Park: Buckeye Trail

It's always great to find a new trail, and the Buckeye Trail in McKinney Roughs Nature Park qualifies, having opened in late 2007. This is really a connector trail between the Road Runner Trail and the Pecan Bottoms Trail, making these trails easier to reach than they were from the main trailhead at the park headquarters. Buckeye Trail passes through the post oak/blackjack oak savanna ecosystem and leads to one of the largest pecan trees in the state. Take the spur off the Road Runner Trail to an overlook of a box canyon and the best view in the park of the Colorado River.

Start: Road Runner trailhead
Nearest town: Austin
Distance: 3-mile loop
Approximate hiking time: 1.5 hours
Difficulty: Moderate due to easy grades
Trail surface: Dirt path, sand
Seasons: September to June
Other trail users: Equestrians, dog walkers
Canine compatibility: Leashed dogs permitted
Land status: Lower Colorado River Authority park
Fees and permits: $3 for adults, $1 seniors, no charge for children 13 and under
Schedule: 8:00 a.m. to 5:00 p.m. daily; day use only

Maps: Trail maps are available in the park office, and also on the Web site www.lcra.org/library/media/public/docs/community_mck_roughs_trailmap.pdf.
Trail contacts: McKinney Roughs Nature Park, 1884 Highway 71 West, Cedar Creek, TX 78612; (512) 303-5073
Other: Check in at the visitor center before hiking, pay your fee, and get a trail map and information. Fee includes the opportunity to borrow one of three nature packs: Birding Pack with binoculars and guidebook; Plant Pack with magnifying glass and explanation of what plants to look for; Kid Pack with bug containers and children's books describing the plants, birds, and insects found at the park.

Finding the trailhead:
From Austin, head east on Highway 71 past Austin-Bergstrom International Airport. Proceed for about 13 miles beyond the airport and look for the park's rock-wall entrance with a windmill on the left (north). Hikers should check in at the Lower Colorado River Authority Park (LCRA) office near the main parking area. The Buckeye trailhead is located at the Pope Bend Equestrian Trail parking area, across the road leading to the Hyatt Regency Resort. From park

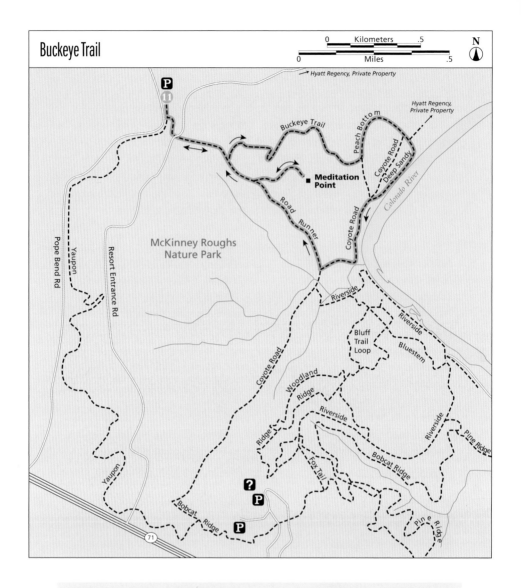

Buckeye Trail

Kilometers 0 — .5

Miles 0 — .5

N

Hyatt Regency, Private Property

Hyatt Regency, Private Property

Buckeye Trail

Peach Bottom

Coyote Road

Deep Sandy

Colorado River

■ **Meditation Point**

Road Runner

Coyote Road

Pope Bend Rd

Yaupon

Resort Entrance Rd

McKinney Roughs Nature Park

Riverside

Riverside

Bluff Trail Loop

Bluestem

Woodland

Ridge

Ridge

Riverside

Riverside

Pine Ridge

Yaupon

Bobcat Ridge

Fox Tail

Bobcat Ridge

Pine Ridge

71

headquarters drive to park entrance and turn right (northwest) onto Highway 71, continue less than a mile and turn right (north) onto Pope Bend Road. Proceed for about a mile to the Pope Bend Equestrian Trailhead parking lot, on your right. DeLorme's *Texas Atlas & Gazetteer*: Page 69 G11. GPS: N30° 92' 700" W97° 27' 484"

THE HIKE

This hike combines sections of the Buckeye, Road Runner, Coyote Road, Deep Sandy, and Pecan Bottom Trails. This northwest section of the park has been maintained in almost pristine condition. Legend has it that bandits used this remote area as a hideout.

A park maintenance person stretches to show how large the circumference of this ancient Pend pecan tree is. The official state tree, this pecan is one of the largest in the state.

Start at the Pope Bend Equestrian Trailhead on the northwest side of McKinney Roughs Nature Park. Follow the Road Runner Trail to the Buckeye Trail and turn left. Enter the woods, which contain several species of oak trees and are part of the post oak savanna ecosystem. There are a few buckeye and hickory trees, but they are hard to find.

Continue bearing generally east on the Buckeye Trail, passing a box canyon to the right. The trail follows the contour of the slightly rolling terrain, making the hiking easier. The trail is shared by equestrians so use caution when going around sharp turns, to avoid spooking the horses of oncoming riders. Horses traveling on the trail after a rain can leave some muddy stretches, but the trail is generally wide enough so these can be skirted.

A visual feast of wildflowers, including Indian Blanket, greets the hiker along many trails.

During May, the woods are full of North America's prettiest birds, the warblers. Seeing a flock of these, containing several species and hundreds of birds, is spectacular. One of the more conspicuous is the yellow warbler, which is the only all-yellow warbler, making it easy to spot and identify. They usually can be heard, if not seen. The male has a high-pitched song: 'Sweet, sweet, I'm so very sweet," generally singing close to his nest 4 to 12 feet off the ground.

Go up and down a few wooded, hilly sections while continuing to head east. The Buckeye Trail descends until it ends at an intersection with the Pecan Bottom Trail. The trail surface becomes sandy as you loop around the moist bottomland. There are more pecan trees, a few mulberry trees, and shrubby undergrowth. Mulberry trees, with their blackberry-like fruit, are a favorite of wildlife.

After making a sweeping right bend and heading southeast, you will see a huge pecan tree. It's impressive and would probably take three men with outstretched arms to circle the trunk. There is a picnic table located nearby where you can rest in the shade.

Continue on down toward the Colorado River, passing Coyote Road on the right. Pecan Bottom ends as it merges onto Deep Sandy Trail, which is appropriately named as the trail surface changes from fairly hard-packed to sand.

Bear southwest, walking along the river where the scenery is totally different from the uplands. The forest has been replaced by the river's flat bottomland and lush growth of bushes and grasses. The temperatures here are 10 to 15 degrees cooler during the summer, giving refreshing relief from the heat. The river's edge is a good place to look for animal signs, including tracks.

After walking about one-third of a mile, Deep Sandy Trail ends where it merges into Coyote Road. Take the left branch, heading south along the river's edge. There are narrow spots on this trail with some overgrowth. Watch for poison ivy.

After bending right and heading away from the river, come to the intersection with Road Runner Trail. Turn right (northwest) onto Road Runner Trail and head up into the woods, going up and down minor grades. Look to the left (southwest) to see some small peaky hills, which are called knobs. The most famous knob in the area is Pilot Knob, the remains of an extinct volcano.

Take the spur on the right (northeast) to a scenic overlook called Meditation Point. The panorama includes a box canyon and the best view of the Colorado River in the park. There are picnic tables and this is a nice place to rest or have a snack. Return to Road Runner Trail, go past the branch with Buckeye Trail, and then backtrack to the trailhead.

0.0   Start at the Road Runner trailhead, following the Road Runner Trail to Buckeye Trail.

0.1   Pass the intersection (actually less than 100 yards) with Yaupon Trail on the right (Yaupon Trail heads south). Continue straight, heading east on Road Runner Trail.

0.1   The Buckeye connector trail intersects the Road Runner Trail on the left (northeast). Turn left onto Buckeye Trail, following the contours of the hills.

0.6   Buckeye Trail ends at the Pecan Bottom Trail. Turn left, heading north and walking in the Colorado River lowlands.

0.9   Pass Coyote Road on right (south) where it intersects Pecan Bottom Trail.

1.0   Pecan Bottom Trail merges onto the Deep Sandy connector to Coyote Road.

1.3   Deep Sandy Trail merges onto Coyote Road. Continue left, heading south on Coyote Road, with the Colorado River on the left (east). Also at this junction, Coyote Road runs north and south and Pecan Bottom Trail connects to Coyote Road from the right (north).

1.8   Travel close to the river, make a right turn heading west and away from the river bottomland, and beginning to climb the slopes. Come to a junction with the Road Runner Trail. Turn right (northwest) onto Road Runner Trail. Coyote Road continues southwest.

2.3   There is a spur on the right (northeast) that leads to Meditation Point. Take the spur. This leads to an overlook that furnishes the best view in the park of the Colorado River. Several picnic benches are located here. Backtrack to Road Runner Trail.

2.8   Turn right (northwest) where the spur intersects Road Runner Trail.

2.9   Pass the intersection on the right (northeast) where the Buckeye connector trail joins Road Runner Trail. Continue west, backtracking on Road Runner Trail to the trailhead.

3.0   End the hike back at the trailhead.

> *The Colorado River, 862 miles long, is the eighteenth longest river in the United States and the longest river with both its source and mouth within Texas.* **Colorado** *means "colored red" in Spanish.*

McKinney Falls State Park: Homestead Trail

The walk to get to the trailhead is a mini-adventure. Go over the lava-like rock flows from Pilot Knob volcano, which created Lower McKinney Falls 80 million years ago. Then ford Onion Creek, or wade across the top of the falls. The trail passes by the ruins of Thomas F. McKinney's 1850s homestead and gristmill. McKinney was of one of the original three hundred colonists in Stephen F. Austin's settlement. Follow Onion Creek, watching for venomous snakes. Return to the trailhead and walk to the Smith Rock Shelter Trail to view the remnants of a natural rock shelter used hundreds of years ago.

Start: Homestead Trail trailhead
Nearest town: Austin
Distance: 3-mile loop
Approximate hiking time: 1.5 hours
Difficulty: Moderate, due to a slight elevation gain and a rocky outcrop
Trail surface: Dirt path with some limestone outcrops
Seasons: September to June
Other trail users: Mountain bikers, joggers, dog walkers
Canine compatibility: Leashed dogs permitted

Land status: State park; Texas Parks & Wildlife Department
Fees and permits: $4 per person or use the State Parks Pass.
Schedule: 8:00 a.m. to 10:00 p.m. daily
Maps: Trail maps are available in the park office. You can also find maps on the Web site www.tpwd.state.tx.us.
Trail contacts: McKinney Falls State Park, 5808 McKinney Falls Parkway, Austin, TX 78744; (512) 243-1643

Finding the trailhead:
From Austin, head south on Highway 183, passing the junctions with Highway 290, and Highway 71. After passing Highway 71, Austin-Bergstrom Airport is on the left (east). McKinney Falls Parkway is on the right (west). There is a brown state park sign that marks the turn. McKinney Falls State Park is about 3 miles from the turn, on the right (north). Enter the park and drive to the park headquarters. Leave the headquarters and take a right, following the park road. Turn right to the Lower McKinney Falls parking area. From here, walk down to the creek and waterfall area. After crossing Onion Creek at the Lower Falls, the trailhead is to the right and marked homestead trail. DeLorme's *Texas Atlas & Gazetteer:* Page 69 G11. GPS: N30° 11' 172" W97° 43' 26"

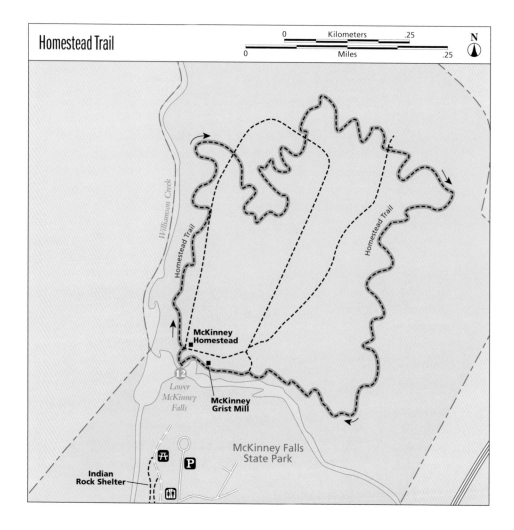

Kilometers   .25

0

Miles   .25

N

Williamson Creek

Homestead Trail

Homestead Trail

McKinney
Homestead

12

Lower
McKinney
Falls

McKinney
Grist Mill

McKinney Falls
State Park

Indian
Rock Shelter

THE HIKE

To start, head left from the parking area, following the northern section of the loop. The trail follows portions of Williamson Creek and Onion Creek; both are important wildlife corridors. Water snakes, including venomous water moccasins, may be near the water's edge. Be careful.

Bear left toward the remains of the Thomas F. McKinney two-story home and some stone fences. The park is named after McKinney, who settled here in the 1850s and became a leading breeder of race horses. He also was one of the original 300 colonists in Stephen F. Austin's early nineteenth-century settlement. As was common for that period, slaves built his home and performed other construction work. Displays near the homestead give more historical information.

Follow the trail as it makes a few turns and then runs parallel with Williamson Creek. Bald cypress, sycamore, buttonbush, and willow trees line the creek bank. The trail is narrow but easy to follow and has thick undergrowth at the edges, where poison ivy can be abundant. Shorebirds may be seen during spring and fall migration.

Bend hard right, going south and away from the creek, then twist and turn with some ups and downs, heading generally northeast. The trail becomes more open and rocky and the Texas Park & Wildlife Department's headquarters complex can be seen to the left. Prickly pear cactus, the Texas state plant, is along the trail edge. Watch for large spider webs woven across the path by orb weavers, a common garden spider.

Wind through a wooded area containing Ashe's juniper, Texas persimmon, and mesquite, while experiencing some slight inclines and declines. In the summer the throaty sound of "chic-breee" may be heard. This is the call of the summer tanager, the only entirely red bird in North America. They nest in the park and their bright red color aids in seeing them chasing wasps and bees.

The park is located at the junction of the Edwards Plateau and the blackland prairie, with the resulting mixed habitats. These include limestone bluffs, creekside thickets, woodlands, mesquite savannas, and brushland; they're home to 224 species of birds and many mammals. The park's landscape is more characteristic of the Edwards Plateau.

Lower McKinney Falls, formed by volcanic action 80 million years ago, is at the junction of Onion Creek and Williamson Creek.

About halfway through the hike, pass a very large live oak. Then go down and across a dry wash and through a large stand of oaks, where the trail crosses a long open stretch of bedrock. Sometimes the limestone forms a stair-stepping topography with sharp dropoffs to the creek. The stabilized remains of the McKinney gristmill now come into view. This was the first mill in the area and was a major contributor to the economy. In August great egrets, a large white bird, can be seen roosting high in the cypress trees, while great blue herons feed along the creek banks.

The terrain leading to Lower Falls was formed 80 million years ago by the eruptions of Pilot Knob volcano, which destroyed nearly everything, but created the Upper and Lower Falls and left many fossils. The fossils of organisms, volcanic debris, and exposed limestone outcroppings along Onion Creek are a snapshot of the Cretaceous period. Backtrack across the Lower Falls and the limestone moonscape back to the parking lot.

After the hike, enjoy the picnic area along Onion Creek. Visit the Rock Shelter Trail, where native Americans roamed hundreds of years ago and archeological excavations have recovered late prehistoric arrow points, bone tools, and other artifacts. The 3.5-mile Onion Creek Hike and Bike Trail loop is also in the park and is wheelchair accessible. The park, although located only 13 miles south of Austin, retains a rustic, out-in-the-woods atmosphere.

MILES AND DIRECTIONS

0.0 Start the Homestead Trail after crossing Onion Creek, then continue to the left, heading north.

0.4 Reach the McKinney Homestead, which is partly hidden by trees. Williamson Creek is on the left (west) and the park maintenance road is on the right (east), but cannot be seen from the trail.

1.1 Cross the park maintenance road and continue heading east.

1.3 Cross the park maintenance road heading north, and then the trail twists and turns and veers sharply right, heading east.

1.5 Go past the park maintenance road junction on the right and continue heading east.

2.3 Veer hard right, heading south.

2.8 Reach the remains of the McKinney gristmill. Continue past the mill back to the trailhead.

3.0 Reach the trailhead, cross the Lower Falls, and return to the parking area.

Nails Creek Unit/Lake Somerville State Park: Flag Pond Loop

Flag Pond Loop is the best for viewing and photographing waterfowl. Viewing areas are located the entire length of the trail. Hike over gently rolling terrain through dense stands of yaupon, post oak, and hickory, and to scenic overlooks and water crossings. Mill Pond Shade Shelter, located on a hill, allows a great view of Flag Pond, a 350-acre improved wetland area that attracts thousands of waterfowl to winter here. One of the best wildflower displays in the Austin area, including Texas blue-bonnet, Indian paintbrush, winecups, and black-eyed Susans, can be seen between mid-March and late April.

Start: Flag Pond Loop trailhead

Nearest town: Somerville

Distance: 5.9-mile loop

Approximate hiking time: 3.5 hours

Difficulty: Moderate due to the length and open canopy

Trail surface: Dirt path, equestrian trail

Seasons: September to June

Other trail users: Equestrians, dog walkers

Canine compatibility: Leashed dogs permitted

Land status: State park; Texas Parks & Wildlife Department

Fees and permits: $2 per person aged 13 and older, or you can use the State Parks Pass.

Schedule: 8:00 a.m. to 5:00 p.m.; day use only

Maps: Trail maps are available in the park office. You can also find maps on the Web site at www .tpwd.state.tx.us.

Trail contacts: Nails Creek & Trailway, 6280 FM 180, Ledbetter, TX 78946-7036; (979) 289-2392. The park is a unit of the Lake Somerville State Park and Trailway.

Other: Parts of the park are subject to flooding, call ahead to see if the trail is open. There are short trails that are wheelchair accessible within the park. A bird checklist is available at the Nails Creek headquarters.

Finding the trailhead:
From Austin take U.S. Highway 290 east to a point about 6 miles east of Giddings. Turn left on FM 180 to the Nails Creek Unit of the Lake Somerville state park complex. Get the combination for the lock on the gate at the Newman Bottom parking area from the ranger. From the Nails Creek headquarters, take FM 180 south to the junction with County Road 125, which is a narrow two-lane asphalt road. Turn right, going east to the junction with County Road 140, which is a rough gravel road. Turn right and head north 7 miles to the

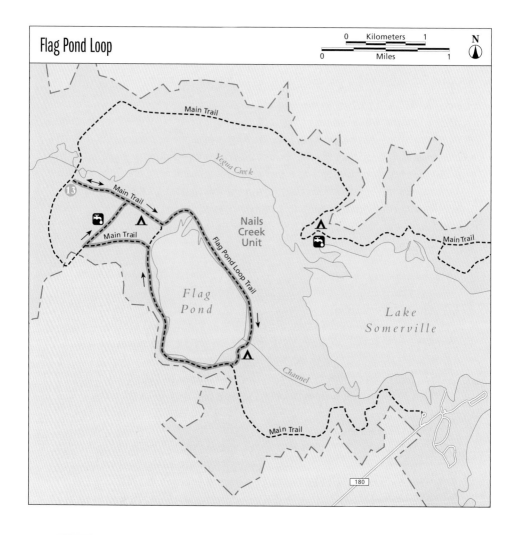

Newman Bottom parking area. A small sign on the right identifies the parking area. The Flag Pond Loop trailhead is adjacent to the parking area. DeLorme's *Texas Atlas & Gazetteer:* Page 70 F5. GPS: N30° 19' 06" W96° 42' 46"

🍃 **Green Tip:**
When hiking with your dog, stay in the center of the path and keep Fido close by. Dogs that run loose can harm fragile soils and spread pesky plants by carrying their seeds.

Lake Somerville is blanketed with characteristic fall morning haze. The lake, located in the Nails Creek Unit of Lake Somerville State Park and Trailway, is the winter home to thousands of ducks.

THE HIKE

The trailhead is reached by walking through the field at the far right corner of the parking lot and heading toward a very large live oak tree. Cross the suspension bridge over Yegua (pronounced "yay wah") Creek and head into the woods.

The Lake Somerville State Park complex contains over 11,000 acres, making it the largest state park in central Texas. There are five units, with the Nails Creek Unit containing 3,155 acres. The units are contiguous and crossed by private ranch roads leading to oil drilling sites. A wrong turn can get you disoriented or lost.

At the junction, take the left segment and go north on the Flag Pond Loop Trail. The Flag Pond Shade Shelter, a small building offering a place to rest, also presents a panoramic view of Flag Pond. Go past post oak, live oak, and yaupon, which is an unwanted invasive tree. A privy and the path to one of the primitive campgrounds are on the right.

At the junction with the Trailway continue right (southwest) around the pond. The terrain is relatively flat and wooded, with a few small hills. Pass an abandoned oil rig; oil-drilling operations are still active in the area. Much of the pond has heavy vegetation, sometimes looking more like a wetland than a pond. The tall bushy grass near the water is bluestem and it likes a wet environment. It is common to see wild hogs here, with as many as twenty in a group. A narrow boat channel on the left leads to Lake Somerville.

The habitat furnishes good cover for quail, which are numerous. Hearing a covey of quail take off can startle even seasoned hunters. The second shade shelter is on the right and has an open view of the pond. Across the park boundary fence to the left (east) of the pond are the Flag Pond Cabins, built by a private hunting club in the late 1920s, when they developed Flag Pond. According to some of the members, the pond got its name because of the American water lotus that grow in it, which were referred to as "flag lilies." The Flag Pond Pavilion, an open-sided building with a clearing between it and the pond, allows a better view of wildlife.

From mid-October to mid-February the sky can be filled with thousands of ducks, mostly gadwells, widgeons, and mallards, as they winter-over on the lake. Fall in central Texas can produce low-hanging ground fog and this combined with the flocks of birds makes a unique picture.

The pond area is also home to the beautyberry, a 6- to 10-foot tall shrub with small purple berries in tight clusters that is abundant and a favorite for wildlife. The trail has one of the best spring wildflower displays in the region, including Texas bluebonnet, the state flower; Indian paintbrush; winecups; golden smoke; black-eyed Susan; and spiderwort.

Pass the shade shelter on the right, on the Trailway. Immediately you will reach a T at the Trailway. Continue straight, and cross a ranch road that leads to an oil company lease. Do not take the ranch road, it could create a lost situation.

Go up a steep hill still in the wooded area, then turn right at the T heading to the Newman Bottom parking area. Pass the shelter that was seen at the beginning of the hike and arrive back at the parking lot.

Newman Bottom was part of the John Newman Ranch. The Lake Somerville Trailway System connects Birch Creek State Park with Nails Creek State Park via 16 miles of multiuse hiking trails.

A black-banded nonvenomous water snake suns itself on a log. Water snakes can be seen along some of the trails that are near creeks, rivers, ponds, and lakes.

MILES AND DIRECTIONS

0.0 Start at the Flag Pond Loop trailhead adjacent to the Newman Bottom parking area.

0.5 Take the left branch, heading east on the Flag Pond Loop.

0.9 Reach Flag Pond, on the right. Continue clockwise around the pond.

2.2 Pass the Mill Pond campground. Pass the T branch with the Trailway. Continue right, going southwest around the pond.

3.7 Reach the shade shelter that overlooks the pond. Follow the trail, which turns and heads northwest.

4.9 Potable water is available at this point. Continue on the trail (the pond is on the right) and head toward the trailhead.

5.9 End the hike back at the trailhead by the Newman Bottom parking area.

Kreische's Bluff Beer

Henry Ludwig Kreische, German immigrant, stonemason, and businessman, in 1849 purchased 172 acres, including a high bluff overlooking the Colorado River and a small deep valley with flowing springs. He then built a three-story, 4,600-square-foot home using native limestone he had quarried.

Several years passed, during which Kreische tried to determine the best use of the valley. Then the idea struck him to build a brewery. Everything was perfect—the valley had flowing springs, there was plenty of stone to construct the brewery, and the Smithville–La Grange Road went right by the site, furnishing a road to town to take his brew to thirsty citizens. The slope of the hill going down to the brewery site was so steep he had to build a set of steps that snaked back and forth to the valley floor. The steps are still in use today.

It then took a bit of ingenuity to figure out how to take advantage of the flow of water and have the pull of gravity work for him. Stone by stone, the 1,800-square-foot brewery was built, containing the brew house, cellars, a lime kiln, and a water supply. Kreische's Bluff Beer was born, produced at the first commercial brewery in Texas.

The brewery operated until shortly after Kreische's death in 1882. The stabilized remains of the Kreische Brewery and the restored home can be seen in the Monument Hill & Kreische Brewery State Historic Sites near La Grange.

Bastrop State Park: Lost Pines and Scenic Overlook Trails

Combine portions of three trails into a 3-mile hike to see the best of Bastrop State Park. Start in the loblolly pines, towering 60 feet overhead. These are part of "Lost Pines," the westernmost stand in Texas, separated from the East Texas piney woods by more than a hundred miles. Go up and down rugged hills and then follow Copperas Creek through a shady forest. In the spring, mating calls from the Houston toad, an endangered species, may be heard. The park was designated a National Historic Landmark in 1997, based on work done in the 1930s by the Civilian Conservation Corps.

Start: Overlook trailhead

Nearest town: Bastrop

Distance: 3.1-mile loop

Approximate hiking time: 2 hours

Difficulty: Moderate due to some steep inclines and narrow paths

Trail surface: Forested dirt path, some rocky sections

Seasons: September to June

Other trail users: Dog walkers

Canine compatibility: Leashed dogs permitted

Land status: State park; Texas Parks & Wildlife Department

Fees and permits: $3 per person for adults 13 years of age and older or use the State Parks Pass. Texas residents age 65 or older pay only $2 per person.

Schedule: 8 a.m. to 10 p.m. daily

Maps: Trail maps are available in the park office. You can also find maps on the Web site www.tpwd .state.tx.us.

Trail contacts: Bastrop State Park, P.O. Box 518/ Highway 21, Bastrop, TX 78602-0518; (512) 321-2101

Other: The Bastrop State Park lake, including the area surrounding it, and the section of the Lost Pines Trail that is east of Harmon Road are closed from February 22 to April 1 to protect the endangered Houston toad during the critical breeding period. Contact Bastrop State Park headquarters at (512) 321-2101 for the latest information. Be aware of eco-sensitive areas.

Finding the trailhead:

Bastrop State Park is located 30 miles east of Austin. From the city take Highway 71 into Bastrop. Turn left at Highway 95 and follow signs to Highway 21. The park entrance is on the left at the intersection of Highways 21 and 71. From the park entrance, follow PR 1A almost 1.5 miles to the Overlook trailhead parking area. DeLorme's *Texas Atlas & Gazetteer*: Page 70 H1. GPS: N30° 06' 451" W97° 16' 883"

THE HIKE

tart the Lost Pines Trail at the Lost Pines Overlook, adjacent to the parking area and across PR 1A. Be sure to look at the brown sandstone shelter at the edge of the parking area, constructed by the CCC in the 1930s and still being used today. Then cross the road and go slightly downhill and immediately into the Lost Pines. These magnificent pines are isolated from the main body of east Texas pines by nearly 100 miles of rolling, post oak woodlands—hence the name Lost Pines. It is part of the most westerly stand of loblolly pines in the state. The 80-foot trees completely dominate and virtually close off all views, while giving total shade. The dried pine needles covering the trail make crunching sounds as they are walked over.

All the trails shown on the Bastrop Park trail map are color-coded: the Lost Pines Trail is purple. This map was completely redone in 2007 when the trails were renamed, and it is one of the finest maps in the system. This hike covers several trails and combines them to make a large loop, covering the most scenic and historic sections of the park.

Go through a gully and across a dry creek bed. Some loose rocks cover parts of the path, and the trail crosses gently rising and falling contours. This short portion of the Lost Pines Trail loop soon comes to the branch with Roosevelt's

Bracken ferns may be found along many of the trails. The ferns, with fronds up to 3 feet long, tend to take over and colonize areas suitable for their growth.

Lost Pines and Scenic Overlook Trails

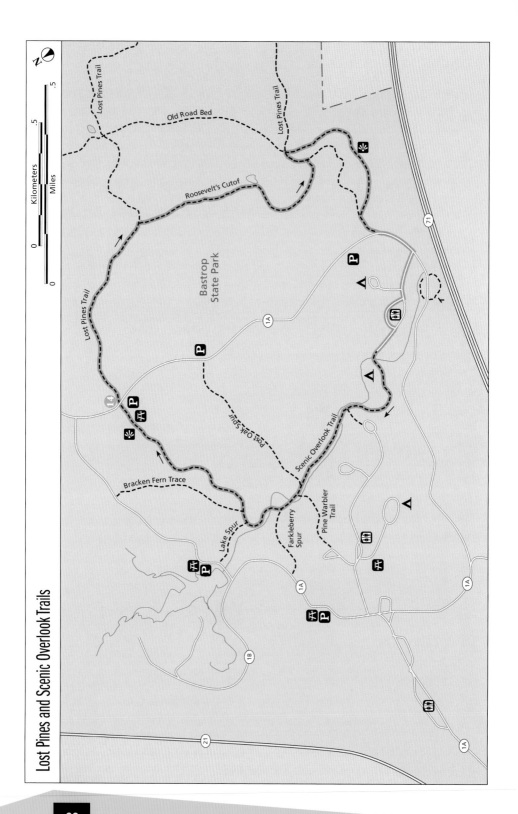

Cutoff, a short connector path (orange on the map). Stay to the right to get on the connector. Head south and watch for the small Toad Pond on the left. Use caution around these ponds as the Houston toad, an endangered species, breeds here. Stay on the marked trails because portions of the park are eco-sensitive, including the ground surface around the base of the shallow-rooted pines.

Make a sweeping right turn and come to an outcrop of sandstone near the connector T into the Lost Pines Trail. Take the right branch, heading south; the left branch heads east and is the south side of the Lost Pines loop. Watch for large groups of bracken fern on both sides of the trail just before it bends right. A gate on the east side of PR 1A marks the end of the Lost Pines Trail.

Cross the road and follow it into the Copperas Creek campground. Copperas Creek is close to the road; a small wooden bridge crosses over it. In April, the dog-woods along the creek are in full bloom. It's possible to see "beggar" raccoons and pairs of dove, recognized by their trilling "coo-coo-coo" song. Water, restrooms, and a shade shelter built by the CCC in the 1930s are available in the campground. The park was designated a National Historic Landmark in 1997 due to the quality work done by the CCC.

At the end of the campground connect with the Scenic Overlook Trail (red on the map), proceeding north. Continue curving slightly left and go past the Piney Hill Spur on the left. Another piece of work done by the CCC lies ahead—a water fountain that at present is nonfunc-tioning. Virginia creeper, a groundcover, can be seen off the trail. This is a good thing because Virginia creeper and poison ivy do not share the same ground. Pass several more branches that lead to other trails. After the last intersecting branch, the Bracken Fern Trace, the Scenic Overlook Trail heads east back to the trail-head. On the fairly steep grade up to the trailhead, Eagle Scouts from Troop 1998 have built erosion fences and water bars.

Over 1,000 species of plants, insects, mammals, and birds reside in the park, gaining it a listing as site HOTE 033 on the Heart of Texas Wildlife Trail. A checklist of the bird species found in the park is available at the park headquarters.

The 13-mile park road that connects Bastrop State Park and Buescher State Park is one of the most scenic woodland drives in Texas.

0.0   Start at the Lost Pines Trail trailhead adjacent to the parking area.

0.3   The trail Ys. Turn right, heading south on the Roosevelt's Cutoff connector trail. The left branch continues the Lost Pines Trail.

0.9   Roosevelt's Cutoff intersects and ends at the Lost Pines Trail at a T intersection. Take the right (south) branch of Lost Pines Trail. The left branch heads east and is part of the Lost Pines Trail loop.

1.5   The Lost Pines Trail ends at Park Road 1A. Continue west and then north on Park Road 1A, passing over Copperas Creek and through the Copperas Creek Campground. There is a brown sandstone rain shelter built by the CCC in the 1930s. There also are restrooms and water here.

1.8   The trail in the campground merges onto the Scenic Overlook Trail. Follow the Scenic Overlook Trail north.

This large sandstone rock is similar to those used by the CCC in the 1930s to build cabins and other park infrastructure.

1.9 Pass the branch to the Piney Hill Spur on the left (west). Continue following the Scenic Overlook Trail, passing a water fountain (not operational) built by the CCC in the 1930s.

2.2 Pass the branch to the Post Oak Spur on the right (east) and almost immediately pass the Pine Warbler Trail on the left (west). Continue on the Scenic Overlook Trail, heading north.

2.3 Pass the Farkleberry Spur on the left (west). Continue heading north for a short distance and then bear right (east).

2.6 Pass the Lake Spur on the left (north), then bear right, heading south and past the Bracken Fern Trace on the left (east), Head south for a short distance and then bear left (east) and follow the Scenic Overlook Trail to the trailhead.

3.1 End the hike at the trailhead and parking area.

The CCC Impact on Parks

"Dad, I'd like to join the CCC and help FDR get the country moving. I'll even be able to send a few dollars home."

These were the sentiments of thousands of young men in the mid-1930s. With the country in the middle of the Great Depression, President Franklin D. Roosevelt established the Civilian Conservation Corps in 1933 to help combat unemployment. Little did he realize the lasting impact the CCC would have on our parks.

The young men working in the program constructed many buildings, trails, and other infrastructure in city parks, state parks, and national parks that are still used today. Men aged seventeen to twenty-three worked in camps of about 200 men each, for six-month periods, where they did outdoor construction work. Few had any work experience beyond odd jobs, and most had completed one year or less of high school. Enrollees worked forty hours a week, were paid $30 a month, and were required to send $25 to their family. Groceries, fuel, equipment, and medical services were contracted locally.

"This is a training station we're going to leave morally and physically fit to lick 'Old Man Depression,'" boasted the newsletter of one of the camps. The CCC became one of the most popular of Roosevelt's New Deal programs and was active in every state.

The availability of labor from the CCC allowed the Texas State Parks Board to develop park lands at a scale not previously attainable. Twenty-seven CCC companies were at work in Texas by 1935, and of the fifty state parks that

▶

received help between 1933 and 1941, thirty-three are still operating. Some of the most notable examples of the work done by the CCC can be seen and used at Bastrop State Park and Palmetto State Park.

"We Get the Job Done" was the motto of Civilian Conservation Corps Camp 873, one of three companies assigned to work in Palmetto State Park. They began in 1934 and finished in October 1935, winning numerous honors for their work. In April 1935 Dr. B. C. Thorpe, a biology professor at the University of Texas, brought his class out to help classify and name 240 of the many different plant species located in the park. Company 873 organized a wildflower show with local groups, adding to the exhibition. It was reported that more than 2,000 visitors attended. The camp newsletter listed numerous activities, including information about programs the townspeople and the CCC members provided for each other.

Palmetto State Park is unique among Texas state parks for its outstanding representation of both the rustic style of its architecture and incorporating natural elements as promoted by the National Park Service.

Bastrop State Park was designated a National Historic Landmark in 1997, based on work done in the 1930s by the CCC. There are fewer than 2,500 of these designations in the country. Construction was done with locally available material—in this case brown sandstone and timber. The park opened in 1937 after roads, culverts, trails, buildings, and other park infrastructure had been completed.

The CCC workforce peaked in August 1935 with 502,000 enrollees in 2,600 camps. The corps was disbanded in 1942 due to World War II. Over three million men had participated. Their work had a lasting impact, still seen and utilized seventy years later.

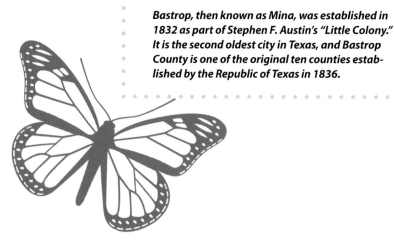

Bastrop, then known as Mina, was established in 1832 as part of Stephen F. Austin's "Little Colony." It is the second oldest city in Texas, and Bastrop County is one of the original ten counties established by the Republic of Texas in 1836.

Monument Hill State Historic Site: Scenic and Historic Trails

This is hiking into history at its best. Following the Kreishe Stairway Trail near the 1850s smokehouse, you'll find 150-year-old retaining walls to the stone remnants of the first commercial brewery in Texas. Hike the 1860s roadbed, with original bridges (culverts) carved from stone. Go up steep hills to the monument to the fifty-eight Texans of the Sommervell/Mier Expedition of 1842. General Santa Anna's execution of seventeen of the captured Texans was one of the events that led to the Mexican War. The view from the bluff overlooking the Colorado River is outstanding.

Start: Monument Hill State Historic Site park headquarters
Nearest town: La Grange
Distance: 1.4-mile loop
Approximate hiking time: 1 hour
Difficulty: Strenuous due to a very steep climb containing switchbacks and the heat, high humidity, and lack of air movement in the valley during the summer
Trail surface: Asphalt, gravel, stone, dirt, and an 1860s roadbed
Seasons: September to May
Other trail users: Dog walkers
Canine compatibility: Leashed dogs permitted
Land status: State Historic Site;

Texas Parks & Wildlife Department
Fees and permits: $4 per person, or use the State Parks Pass.
Schedule: 8:00 a.m. to 5:00 p.m. daily
Maps: Trail maps are available in the park office. You can also find maps on the Web site www.tpwd .state.tx.us.
Trail contacts: Monument Hill State Historic Site, 414 State Loop 92, La Grange, TX 78945; (979) 968-5658
Other: Guided tours of the brewery and home are available by calling the park office.

Finding the trailhead:
From Austin head east on Highway 71. Proceed into La Grange, turn right onto Highway 77, and head south. Turn right onto Spur 92, go 0.4 mile, and look for the park headquarters and parking area on the right. Check in at park headquarters, get a map, and ask for the combination to the lock on the gate at the trailhead for Kreishe Stairway Trail. DeLorme's *Texas Atlas & Gazetteer:* Page 70 I13. GPS: N29° 53' 284" W96° 52' 573"

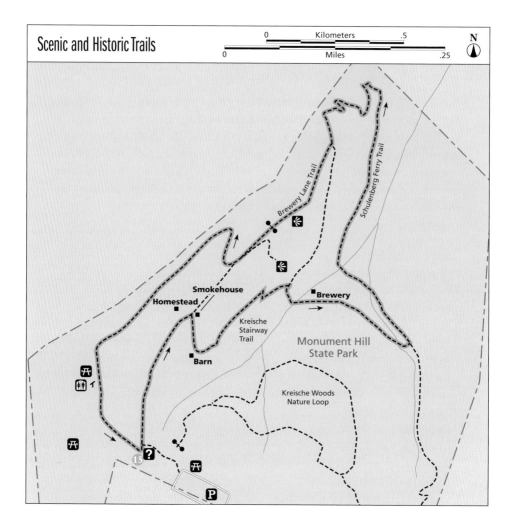

Scenic and Historic Trails

Brewery Lane Trail

Schulenberg Ferry Trail

Smokehouse
Homestead

Brewery

Kreische
Stairway
Trail

Monument Hill
State Park

Barn

Kreische Woods
Nature Loop

THE HIKE

t's great to find a newly created trail that is also steeped in history. The hike combines the Kreishe Stairway Trail, the Scenic and Historic Trail, and the Schulenberg Ferry Trail, which was developed in late 2007. The addition of the Schulenburg Ferry Trail makes this state historic site a great hiking destination.

From the Monument Hill State Historic Site park headquarters, take the right branch of the wheelchair-accessible Scenic and Historic Trail. This leads past the restored Kreische family home on the left and the smokehouse on the left behind you. The trail branches at the smokehouse. Take the right branch that leads to the Kreische Stairway Trail. A locked gate blocks the path and must be opened before proceeding.

There are several benches with shade provided by trees on the path to the brewery. Spanish moss drapes the trees and several wild grapevines twine up the oak trees. This section has the hand-hewn steps and retaining walls constructed by German immigrant, stone-mason, brewer, and businessman H. L. Kreische. There are a number of switchbacks leading to the valley floor, which makes walking down the steep slope easier. The stabilized remains of the brewery, one of the first commercial breweries in Texas, can be seen from several observation platforms. Much of the building was destroyed by floods and vegetation, but large sections of the stone walls and some of the rooms remain. Kreische's Bluff Beer was produced here.

Pass around the brewery, which has restricted access, and head east, going up into an oak and cedar forest that provides welcome shade. Look for white-tailed deer tracks on the trail and for deer paths leading into the woods. This section of the trail, named Brewery Lane Trail, intersects with the Schulenburg Ferry Trail at the Upper Bridge.

Schulenburg Ferry Trail resembles a jeep trail and is the remnant of the 1860s Smithville–La Grange highway. Take the left branch and head toward the Lower Bridge. The right branch connects with the Kreische Woods Nature Loop. There are no bridges at the Upper and Lower Bridge, just stone culverts near a

The stabilized remains of the Kreische Brewery are located in Monument Hill State Historic Site. The brewery, built in the 1860s from hand-hewn stones, is reputed to be the first commercial brewery in Texas.

creek that kept the wagons from getting mired down. They were called bridges during the 1800s.

Hiking in the valley can be extremely hot and humid due to the lack of airflow, so take adequate water. The trail is wide but there are some steep dropoffs along the edge, so use caution. Go through oak woods and little-bluestem prairies, which are intermixed throughout the park. Continue as the trail bears sharply left and climbs west through a series of very steep switchbacks. The route rises from the valley floor to the top of the 200-foot bluff overlooking the Colorado River. This is the most difficult part of the hike and may not be suitable for young children.

The Schulenburg Ferry Trail ends at a Y. Take the right leg, which is the paved Brewery Lane Trail and passes the Lower Bluff Overlook. Continue a short distance to a kiosk where Brewery Lane Trail ends at the Scenic and Historic Trail loop. Bear right to the edge of the bluff and a scenic overlook of the river valley and the city of La Grange. The river valley soils contain sandstone, and "eastern" flora and fauna coexist with the limestone-loving "western" species from 70 miles northwest, deposited in the area by the river.

The paved wheelchair-accessible path leads to the monument honoring the seventeen Texans who were executed by General Santa Anna in 1843. It is a large noble monument, with the remains of the soldiers buried beneath it. Return to the parking lot.

MILES AND DIRECTIONS

0.0   Start at the park headquarters and head north on the Scenic and Historic Trail.

0.1   Reach the Kreishe Stairway trailhead.

0.3   Reach the Upper Bridge after following the steep steps down into the valley and passing the remains of the brewery. The bridge is just a stone culvert. Turn left at the Upper Bridge on the Schulenburg Ferry Trail, heading northwest.

0.4   Pass the Lower Bridge (also just a stone culvert), and then cross a seasonal creek.

0.6   Reach the start of a steep series of switchbacks. This is the most difficult section of the hike. Bear sharply left and then left again, following the trail south.

0.8 Reach the top of the switchbacks and the top of the bluff. The path is now paved and the paths to the Brewery Overlook, Scenic Overlook, and the Scenic and Historic Trail around the monument area, are in your line of sight. Continue southwest, selecting your own route to the park office.

1.4 Reach the park office and the end of the hike.

Local information
For information on La Grange contact the La Grange Chamber of Commerce, 171 South Main, La Grange, TX 78945. The chamber is housed in the 1883 structure that served as the county jail for Fayette County for over one hundred years. Call (800) 524-7264; the Web site is www.lagrangetx.org.

The Black Bean Incident

It was a typical fall day in La Grange, Texas, in 1843. The local men who had gathered under the "Muster Oak" (one of the "Famous Trees of Texas" and still standing) were talking about signing up with Captain Nicholas Dawson for the Somervell-Mier Expedition to fight Mexican troops. The Texas settlers were rebelling against new rules imposed by Mexico. Little did they imagine that within weeks they would be captured by Mexican general Santa Anna.

As the Texas force entered and then left the town of Mier, the Mexican army's First Division, North Corps, was sent to stop them. General Pedro de Ampudia, in charge of the First Division, had already captured two of the Texans, who told him their group was about to reenter Mier. Ampudia then quickly and silently occupied the town, setting up two small cannons and several lines of defense, including snipers on rooftops.

On February 25, the Texans attacked, only to be greeted by a barrage of enemy fire. After a spirited battle, the men under Captain Dawson were surrounded by overwhelming numbers of the enemy. A Mexican courier was sent under a white flag to tell Dawson he had one hour to surrender or be annihilated. He chose to surrender and, according to a letter from Ampudia to his superiors, ". . . the haughty conquerors started to march past in platoons, deposited their rifles, pistols, and daggers on the ground, in front of the unconquered and faithful defenders."

The captured men were marched to Saltillo, Mexico, to be imprisoned. They attempted escape, but within a day, all 176 men were recaptured. Santa Anna was furious, ordering General Meheir to shoot every escapee. The general refused on the grounds "he would not be a murderer" and was removed from his position by Santa Anna. It is said that the foreign ministers of France and

▶

Britain were asked by the United States government to intervene, and it was then that Santa Anna decided only one man out of ten would be executed.

One hundred seventy-six beans were counted into an earthen jar; seventeen were black. First, each commissioned officer was to draw a bean followed by the enlisted men. Those with black beans would be shot, the others would be jailed. At dusk on March 25, 1843, the seventeen men were brought into a courtyard to be executed. Sixteen were killed instantly, while the seventeenth, James Shepherd, fell to the ground wounded in the arm and pretended to be dead. The guards left him for dead, and he escaped that night, finding a shepherd who allowed him to use his home to recover. He then carelessly went into the town of Saltillo, where he was recognized as the escaped Texan and was shot and killed on the street.

This event became known as the Black Bean Incident. In combination with Santa Anna's order to "give no quarter" at the Alamo and his victory there, the Black Bean Incident rallied the people living in Texas, leading to the U.S.–Mexican war of 1846–1848. The U.S. triumph resulted in the annexation of Texas to the United States.

In 1848 the remains of sixteen of the seventeen victims of the Black Bean Incident, and forty-two other combatants of that era, were returned from Mexico and buried on a bluff overlooking the Colorado River and the town of La Grange. A large monument was erected in their honor. The site is now part of Monument Hill & Kreische Brewery State Historic Sites.

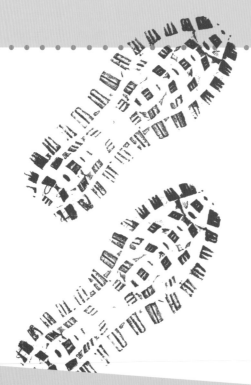

Jackrabbits scamper around a windmill, many of which are still in operation in Central Texas.

San Antonio, the nation's ninth largest city, is situated 70 miles southwest of Austin at the intersection of Interstate Highways 10, 35, and 37. It is a gateway to the Hill Country to the west. Along with Austin, the city is within the Balcones Escarpment and sits on the eastern edge of the Edwards Plateau. San Antonio is 650 feet above sea level.

The Edwards Plateau is a high, hundred-mile-long section of land. Millions of years of erosion have shaped the plateau into a hilly, rocky terrain, with major rivers still cutting new paths. Deep underground is the Edwards Aquifer, which stores billions of gallons of water and is the sole source of drinking water for the city as well as furnishing water for creeks, rivers, and wildlife. San Antonio is the largest American city whose main water source is an aquifer.

The Balcones Escarpment was created 40 million years ago and runs through the eastern half of the city and up through Austin. The Spanish explorers called the area *Balcones,* meaning "balcony," because the alternating layers of hard and soft limestone gave the appearance of a balcony or stair steps. This uplift formed an area with many springs, steep canyons, valleys, and limestone outcrops, making hiking interesting, scenic, and sometimes challenging. San Antonio has taken advantage of this geology to create some

Limestone outcropping and scrub cedar are common sights on many of the trails.

outstanding parks and hiking trails, which include Friedrich Natural area (hike 29), Medina River Natural area (hike 30), and McAllister Park (hike 26). Almost within sight of the city, two other areas have been preserved. Hill Country State Natural Area (hikes 19 and 20) and Government Canyon State Natural Area, opened in 2007 (hikes 24 and 25) and both in the Hill Country, provide miles of trails.

This uplift formed ... many springs, steep canyons, valleys, and limestone outcrops, making hiking interesting, scenic, and sometimes challenging.

The San Antonio River, which originates in San Antonio, has opportunities for both historical and nature hikes with the Missions Trail and RiverWalk (hikes 27 and 28). This shared geology is the glue that holds Austin, San Antonio, and the adjoining Hill Country together to make it great hiking country.

San Antonio was named by Spanish missionaries, who founded the city on St. Anthony's Day in 1718. Spain then established missions along an 8-mile, north-south stretch of the San Antonio River. Mission San Antonio de Valero (the Alamo, 1718), Mission Concepción (1731), Mission San José (1720), Mission San Juan Capistrano (1731), and Mission San Francisco de la Espada (1741), make up the San Antonio Missions National Historical Park (hike 28), one of a few urban national parks in the country. American Indians lived along the San Antonio River, calling the vicinity *Yanaguana,* meaning "refreshing waters." San Antonio is the only major Texan city founded before Texas won its independence from Mexico.

Spanish, Mexican American, European (German, Swiss, and Czech), and southern United States influences have formed a unique "Texan" culture, giving the city a rich, if complex, nature.

Best known for the Alamo and the RiverWalk or "Paseo del Rio," San Antonio offers an unusual variety of hikes for those who love the outdoors, as well as history buffs.

Palmetto State Park offers three excellent short trail options that can be hiked separately or during a single outing. East and west Texas ecosystems meet up on these trails. The Palmetto Trail conjures scenes from the film Jurassic Park, *with clinging vines, dwarf palmettos, green ponds, and a variety of insects in the Ottine Swamp. The four-acre oxbow lake, formed by the meandering San Marcos River and visited via the Lake Trail, offers a variety of vegetation and possibly some water snakes. The Hiking Trail takes you under a dense forest cover to an operating hydraulic ram-jet pump built in 1935 by the Civilian Conservation Corps. Palmetto State Park is a stop on Texas Parks and Wildlife's Great Texas Birding Trail.*

Nearest town: Gonzales
Distance: 3.4 miles for all three
Approximate hiking time: 2.25 hours total
Difficulty: Easy for all three trails, due to the level terrain and good shade
Trail surface: Dirt
Seasons: Year-round
Other trail users: Dog walkers
Canine compatibility: Leashed dogs permitted

Land status: State park, Texas Parks & Wildlife Department
Fees and permits: $4 per person or use the State Parks Pass.
Schedule: 8:00 a.m. to 10:00 p.m. daily
Maps: Trail maps are available in the park office. You can also find maps on the Web site www.tpwd .state.tx.us.
Trail contacts: Palmetto State Park, 78 Park Road 11 South, Gonzales, TX 78629; (830) 672-3266

Finding the trailhead:
To reach the park from Gonzales, travel 10 miles northwest on U.S. Highway 183 to Farm Road 1586. Go west on FM 1586 for 2 miles to Ottine, then south on PR 11 for 2 miles to park headquarters. DeLorme's *Texas Atlas & Gazetteer:* Page 78 A5. GPS: N29° 35' 22" W97° 34' 92"

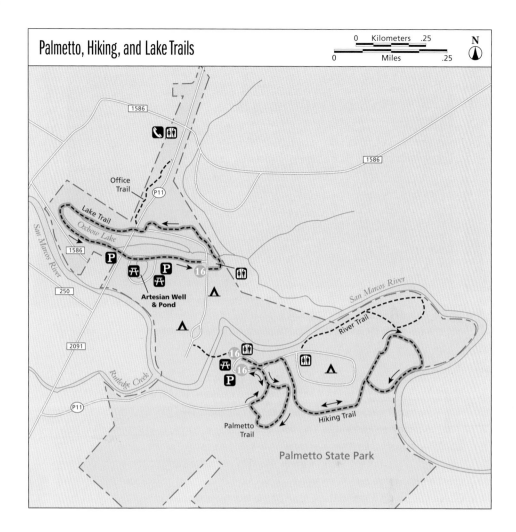

PALMETTO TRAIL

Start: Palmetto Trail trailhead
Distance: 0.3-mile lollipop

Approximate hiking time: 0.5 hour

Finding the trailhead:
Follow directions to the park. The trailhead is adjacent to PR 11, a short distance east and south of the Refectory parking lot. GPS: N29° 35' 237" W97° 34' 566"

A green-colored pond in Palmetto State Park is surrounded by dwarf palmettos, vines, and trees that add to the *Jurassic Park*–like atmosphere on the Palmetto Trail.

THE HIKE

This is a self-guided trail with numbered markers, which are referenced in an interpretive guide available near the trailhead. This flat, well-marked trail is wheelchair accessible. The shift in elevation is nominal, but the shift in vegetation is remarkable. This short walk is the signature hike of the park.

Pass several plant identification markers near the start of the trail and then cross a footbridge over a swampy area. A sign on the left tells about the hydraulic ram-jet pump located there, one of the few operational ram-jet pumps in existence. This pump uses no electricity—instead, the energy of water flowing from an artesian well moves the water from below ground to the water storage tower. The brown sandstone storage tower, partially obscured by trees, is an impressive building. The water supplied by the pumping system has helped the swamp, palms, flowers, and forest to survive after the water table had been lowered by the pumping of water and oil. The jet pump, water tower, Refectory (communal dining hall), and other buildings and infrastructure in the park were constructed by the Civilian Conservation Corps in 1937.

Thick stands of dwarf palmettos, only 3 to 4 feet tall, are on the right and left of the trail. These palms, with their large fan-shaped leaves, serve as the understory for larger trees. Spaced between ephemeral lagoons, they cause thoughts of *Jurassic Park*. This is the Ottine Swamp, with its lush growth and numerous seasonal ponds, some where the water has turned pea-green. Because of this landscape, Palmetto State Park resembles the tropics more than central Texas. The dwarf palmetto is more common along the Gulf Coast from Louisiana to Florida.

Heavy tree cover shades the entire path and subdues the light. This, along with the gray Spanish moss trailing through the branches of live oak, green ash, and other trees, adds to the eerie impression. There are small ponds on each side, with palmettos growing at their edge.

Pass a gully on the right, go by a large sycamore tree dressed with a trumpet vine with bright orange flowers, and then cross a footbridge over a narrow dry creek bed. In the fall, American goldfinches and yellow-bellied sapsuckers are among the 240 bird species that can be seen in the park.

Pass some burr oak trees, which are easily identified in the fall by the large acorns with a fringe around the cap that are scattered on the ground. The palmettos are still on all sides and in August bear small spheres of fruit. Eastern and western Texas species merge here, resulting in an astounding diversity of plant and animal life.

The loop ends back at PR 11, and from there backtrack to the parking lot. On returning to the parking lot, be sure to visit the Refectory and pavilion behind it. These overlook the San Marcos River and are a great spot for a picnic.

HIKING TRAIL

Start: Hiking Trail trailhead
Distance: 2.4-mile lollipop
Approximate hiking time: 1 hour
Other: The trail is not well-marked, and many paths have been made by campers. Water moccasins and rattlesnakes, both venomous, are in the park, but are seldom seen and rarely encountered.

Finding the trailhead:
Follow directions to the park from Gonzales to park headquarters. The trailhead is a short distance east of the Refectory parking lot and adjacent to PR 11. DeLorme's *Texas Atlas & Gazetteer:* Page 78 A5. GPS: N29° 35' 237" W97° 34' 566"

THE HIKE

On this hike you'll see the remnants of hot springs, which in the 1930s people thought provided a cure for polio. Starting from the trailhead, pass a small clearing where a few dwarf palmettos are growing beneath taller trees. The woods continue for the balance of the hike and furnish welcome shade.

After completing a couple of turns, come to a sign on the left that indicates the presence of a mud boil. Look hard—there is no boiling mud, just a wet depression in the ground near the sign. Prior to the 1970s, this area was wetter and had more thermal activity, including hot springs that created mud boils. This activity probably

A water tower in Palmetto State Park was constructed by the Civilian Conservation Corps in the mid-1930s from native sandstone. The CCC was established by President Franklin D. Roosevelt to provide work for young men during the Great Depression.

ended due to changes brought about by the widespread drilling for oil and water. At the turn of the twentieth century, the swamp was a major attraction to visitors seeking the healing powers of the hot springs. The Warm Springs Foundation in Ottine was established in 1937 to use the waters in the treatment of polio. Many artesian wells and flowing springs can still be found in the park today.

The trail squiggles around and the terrain remains flat. Head east past the south side of the modern camping area and skirt campsites 9 to 19. Heavy woods and undergrowth keep the campground from view. Although raccoons are normally nocturnal animals, a few "beggars" may be seen gathering food near the campground. The palmettos have all but disappeared here; they've been replaced by oak, elm, and hackberry trees. Stray paths intercept the trail. Pass a gully on the right and continue right as another stray path branches off.

The trail veers to the right and heads into a marshy area near the river. This is an area alive with sound, including the hum of insects, the beeping of frogs, and the calls of numerous birds being heard, but not seen.

At the next branch take the right leg, which leads to a short, but steep grade. This is the first minor change in elevation. The campground is on the right and several paths lead to campsite 9. At the top of the incline, continue straight and backtrack to the trailhead.

MILES AND DIRECTIONS

0.0 Start at the Hiking Trail trailhead, located a short distance east of the Refectory parking lot and adjacent to PR 11.

0.9 Reach the junction where the Hiking Trail loop connects to itself. Turn right, heading southeast. Follow the loop around, bearing left.

1.5 Return to the junction where the Hiking Trail loop connects. Backtrack toward the trailhead.

2.4 End the hike back at the trailhead.

LAKE TRAIL

Start: Lake Trail trailhead
Distance: 0.7-mile loop

Approximate hiking time: 0.75 hour

Finding the trailhead:
Follow directions to the park. To reach the Lake Trail trailhead from PR 11, take the first turn left into the campground area, heading east. Go to the parking lot by the restrooms, next to campsite 26. The trailhead is behind the restrooms. DeLorme's *Texas Atlas & Gazetteer:* Page 78 A5. GPS: N29° 35' 22" W97° 34' 92"

THE HIKE

Lake Trail is a short walk that affords the opportunity to see an oxbow lake, many animal tracks, and a variety of trees and insects. In the spring, damselflies, dragonflies, butterflies, sulphur moths, and mosquitoes are abundant from ground level to head height. Nonvenomous water snakes may be seen around the Lake and River Trails.

From the trailhead, you'll immediately go into a swampy, wooded area, then slightly downhill and left to a wooden bridge. After crossing the bridge, stay left past some swampland. Cross another bridge over wetlands and then the trail meanders through woods, past oak and elm trees. Oxbow Lake can be seen about 30 yards to the left. The four-acre lake was created when the slow-moving San Marcos River changed directions and left an isolated lagoon. Deer tracks, almost heart-shaped, are common as the deer cross the trail headed to the lake.

Oxbow Lake was formed by the changing course of the San Marcos River.

Come into a grassy area that has five upright posts to block traffic. Cross PR 11 and continue over a mowed area, with Oxbow Lake on the left. Turn left where the trail branches, the right leg leads to the park office.

Cross a bridge over a swampy area. Thirty yards ahead is another foot bridge that crosses an overflow channel from the lake. Continue straight ahead, with the shoreline about 20 feet away on the left, and go past heavy growth, including poison ivy. As the trail turns right and left, but stays close to lake's edge, the number of trees decreases. Small openings onto the lakeshore offer an opportunity to see deer, armadillo (the state's official small mammal), and raccoon tracks by the water's edge. Although the park has a variety of mammals, white-tailed deer, squirrels, and armadillo are most likely to be seen during daylight.

The trail wanders away from the lake and then heads back to a long clearing that extends to the water's edge. This gives an opportunity to observe various water insects, including water striders. A good view of the entire lake can be seen from here.

Make a bend left and head south, continuing on the loop around the lake. Go past some large wild grapevines on both sides of the trail, climbing high into the trees. Watch for low-hanging tree branches and spiderwebs. Bear left, staying close to the lakeshore; although FM 1586 is about 20 feet away on the right, there is little traffic to disturb the hike. The Little Hill Baptist Church is ahead and to the right.

Continue straight and cross under the PR 11 bridge that spans the lake. On the other side of the bridge, there is a large sign warning about snakes. This area seems to be a favorite place for water snakes, including venomous water moccasins, to sun themselves along the trail.

Follow the trail east skirting the picnic area and past campground sites 20 to 24, to the parking lot. In August at dusk, the path is alive with the blinking orange and yellow lights of fireflies.

MILES AND DIRECTIONS

0.0 Start at the Lake Trail trailhead, located to the left and behind the restrooms next to campsite 26. Follow the trail counter-clockwise.

0.2 Cross PR 11 at the bridge. Continue following the loop along the lake, going generally west and then curving around the end of the lake to head east.

0.3 Cross PR 11 at the bridge. Continue past the play field and campsites, heading for the parking lot.

0.7 End the hike back at the parking lot.

Oxbow Lake on the San Marcos River

As the San Marcos River meandered through the area around the Ottine Swamp near Gonzales, it cut a deeper waterway. As this was happening, some layers of soil and rock below its path became harder. The slow-moving river could not easily erode the material attempting to block its flow, so it chose the easy course and cut away into a new, softer channel. Since the river traveled slower on the inside of the curve, depositing silt, and the flow on the outside was faster, causing erosion, a loop was formed.

As the loop, now shaped like an oxen yoke or bow, grew to about five times the width of the San Marcos, the water flow began eroding the neck. The loop was now isolated as the river formed a new course. This was the beginning of the oxbow lake. Over time, sediment will fill the shallow lake. Without a supply of water, in a process known as succession, the lake will become a wetland, then a meadow, and then a forest. Oxbow Lake in Palmetto State Park is one of the finest examples in Texas.

17

Kerrville–Schreiner Park: Red, Green, Orange Trails

This hike snakes across rolling Ashe's juniper-covered terrain and combines portions of the Red, Green, and Orange Trails with the Old Road Trail to experience the best in the park. White-tailed deer are abundant in the park and their paths crisscross the trail. An overlook on the Orange Trail gives a great view of the Guadalupe River valley. Live oak, Spanish oak, buckeye, and pecan trees are plentiful. Wildflowers, particularly the Texas bluebonnet, the state flower, are abundant in spring. The endangered golden-cheeked warbler and black-capped vireo may be seen from April to July.

Start: Trailhead 2
Nearest town: Kerrville
Distance: 3.2 miles; interconnecting loops
Approximate hiking time: 2.0 hours
Difficulty: Strenuous due to the steep grades and rocky sections on the Orange Trail
Trail surface: Dirt, limestone outcrops
Seasons: Year-round
Other trail users: Dog walkers
Canine compatibility: Leashed dogs permitted
Land status: City park; City of Kerrville
Fees and permits: $4 for adults and youths 13 to 64 years old; $2 for those over 64 years old
Schedule: 8:00 a.m. to 10:00 p.m. daily
Maps: Trail maps are available in the park office. You can also find maps on the Web site www.tpwd.state.tx.us; click on the link on the Kerrville–Schreiner page.
Trail Contacts: Kerrville–Schreiner Park, 2385 Bandera Highway, Kerrville, TX 78028; (830) 257-5392
Other: You will need to get a permit and the combination for the lock on the gate at park headquarters. This site operated by the city of Kerrville is not part of the state park system.

Finding the trailhead:
From Kerrville take Highway 16 southwest to Highway 173 and proceed for 3 miles. The park headquarters is on the east side of Highway 173 at 2385 Bandera Highway; the trails are on the west. Hikers must stop at headquarters to sign in and get the combination to the lock on the entrance gate. Trailhead 2 is between the Mountain View and High Point camping loops, located across Highway 173 and the park headquarters. Cross the highway and head to the right, passing Trailhead 1 and the Mountain View campground to the Trailhead 2 parking area. DeLorme's *Texas Atlas & Gazetteer:* Page 68 I3. GPS: N30° 29' 931" W98° 13' 100"

THE HIKE

This hike combines sections of the Red, Green, Orange, and Old Road trails to give a sampling of the Hill Country landscape including hills, ridges, and arroyos. These are interconnecting loops, so adjustments can be made to shorten, lengthen, or change directions. Look for white-tailed deer in the woods along the edge of the trail, especially in the early morning and late afternoon.

The park has an unusual history. It was constructed as a city park in the mid-1930s by the Civilian Conservation Corps, a work program initiated by President Franklin D. Roosevelt to reduce unemployment during the Great Depression. The State of Texas later acquired the park and it became part of the Texas Parks & Wildlife Department system. In February 2004 the park was transferred back to the city of Kerrville. What goes around, comes around.

Start the Red Trail at Trailhead 2, and immediately enter a cedar forest. Continue straight and slightly up, past scattered rocks. Pass a branch on the left and almost immediately come to an intersection with the connector leading to the west side of the Red Trail loop. Turn left and go a very short distance to meet the loop, taking the right leg north. Go down a set of steps. A deer path crosses the trail and leads past the cedars into a small clearing.

Bend to the left and then to the right. At the Y take a hard left and follow the connector until it joins the Green trail. At the junction take a hard right, go up a set of steps, and bend left, going west. This sounds complicated, but it's interesting and happens quickly.

Limestone rocks, overhanging tree branches, and cactus decorate
Kerrville-Schreiner City Park.

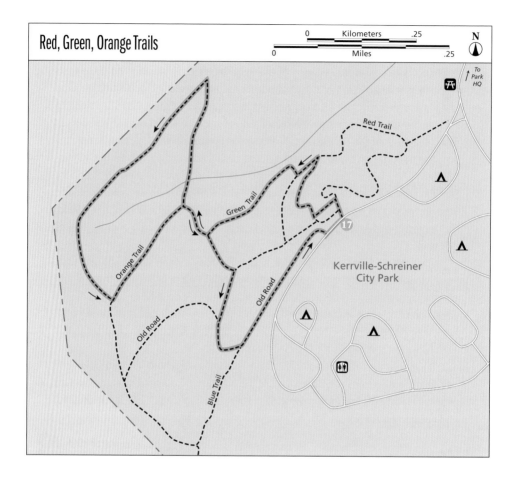

Continue straight and up a small hill, past scattered rocks, to a branch. Turn right and travel to a Y that connects the east and west loops of the Orange Trail. Some erosion has occurred even though there are 8-inch-square water bars across the trail.

Turn left, going west along a wooded valley with juniper, live oak, and pecan trees. At the junction make a right turn, heading north to stay on the Orange Trail. This section is steep, rocky, and uphill, with little tree cover, and the most strenuous part of the hike. It may be excluded by staying on the Green Trail, which is one of the advantages of interconnecting loop trails. Limestone outcroppings and scattered rock abut the trail.

The trail goes steadily uphill until there is a slight curve heading right that leads to an overlook. On the left is a sweeping view of the Guadalupe River valley and a residential area. A large water tower is on the left and marks the park boundary.

Start heading down, walking close to the park's northern boundary fence. The trail is strewn with small rocks and gravel, making the descent only a little less strenuous than hiking up the hill. It's possible to see the endangered golden-cheeked warbler and black-capped vireo here from April to July.

The grade becomes easier and there are fewer rocks on the trail. Continue down to a very sharp right bend, heading southwest and away from the park's east boundary. Come to the intersection with the connector trail and turn left, following the valley to a Y with the Green Trail. Take the right leg and follow it to the intersection with the Old Road Trail.

Go left at the intersection; the trail becomes a flat, wide gravel road. Curve left and come to a branch, staying left on the Old Road Trail and following it to the gate at Trailhead 2.

Additional hiking is available on the Wooden Post and Yellow Trail. Portions of the Yellow trail are wheelchair accessible from Trailhead #3.

Note: Trail branches are identified with 4-foot-high trail markers that have color-coded arrows (the arrows are the color of the trail name) pointing to the direction of travel.

MILES AND DIRECTIONS

0.0   Start the Red Trail at Trailhead 2 parking area.

0.1   Pass the T intersection with the Green Trail. Turn left (west) at the Red Trail connector and follow it a short distance to where it Ts into the Red Trail. Turn right, going northwest, and immediately come to a set of steps. Follow the trail as it bends left and then right.

0.2   Reach the Y branch with the Green Trail. Turn left, heading east. In a short distance the Green Trail loop Ts into itself. Turn right and immediately go down a set of steps. Then follow the trail veering left (east).

0.6   Reach the Y branch with the Orange Trail. Turn right, heading northeast onto the Orange Trail. **Note:** The Orange Trail has some steep, uphill, stony sections. This is the most difficult part of the hike. This section can be eliminated by turning left at this branch onto the Green Trail.

1.0   Reach the branch where the Orange Trail loop intersects a leg of a connector trail to the Old Road Trail. Turn right, heading north, and start a steady climb to the top of the valley.

1.4   On the top of the hill come to an overlook where a sweeping view of the Guadalupe River valley is available. Follow the trail down as it heads northeast and parallels the fence marking the park boundary.

2.1 After veering hard right, going south, come to the branch where the Orange Trail loop connects to itself. Turn left (southeast) and head for the Green Trail.

2.2 Reach the Y branch with the Green Trail; the Orange Trail ends. Turn right, continuing southeast.

2.3 Reach the Y branch where the Green Trail Loop connects to itself. Turn right, heading south on the short Green Trail connector to the Old Road Trail.

2.4 The Green Trail connector ends at the Old Road Trail. Turn left and follow the Old Road Trail, a wide flat path.

Fawns are easy to see in spring, feeding along the edges of trails. Early morning and late afternoon are the best times to spot them.

2.5 Follow the Old Road as it bends to the left. Come to the branch where the Blue Trail, coming from the right, connects and ends at the Old Road Trail. Continue left, following the Old Road Trail toward the trailhead.

3.2 End the hike at the gate to Trailhead 2 parking area.

Local Information
For information about Kerrville contact the Kerrville Convention and Visitors Bureau, 2108 Sidney Baker Suite 200, Kerrville, TX 78028; (830) 792-3535; www.kerrvilletexascvb.com.

Wild Camels Seen in Texas

Wild camels roaming in central Texas? Preposterous, but those were the rumors circulating in the 1870s. The tales were based on the fact that Camp Verde, near Bandera, was selected as the base for the U.S. Army's experiment in using camels for transportation. About seventy-five camels were based there as part of the U.S. Camel Corps, and from 1855 to 1869 they were part of the U.S. Cavalry.

After Texas was ceded to the United States at the end of the Mexican War, the U.S. government was encouraging pioneers to settle in the new territory. The army began establishing more forts in the Southwest to protect the settlers. Supplies were sent to the forts by wagonloads, which were pulled by horses and mules. These animals required food and water, which meant the army either had to maintain outposts a day's journey apart or carry the extra forage and water in additional wagons. This was very expensive and typically slowed the journey.

A variety of alternatives were considered, and the army decided to experiment with camels. This created, on August 26 and 27, 1856, the strangest caravan that ever crossed Bandera Pass, 12 miles south of Kerrville—a herd of camels on the final leg of their trip from the Middle East to Camp Verde.

Trying to find other uses for the camels, they were trained to race in 1860, hoping a "camel express" mail service could be formed. But the camels, excellent in carrying heavy loads, could not compete with horses in this regard. The remaining camels in the army's Camel Corps were sold in the late 1860s. Part of the problem was that the rocky terrain of the Southwest had damaged their feet. Rumor has it that some of these animals were turned loose or escaped, thus supporting the stories of wild camels in Texas.

Lost Maples State Natural Area: East Trail

After scrambling for a mile over, around, and up limestone outcroppings deceptively called steps, you can view the Sabinal River and canyon from the canyon's ridgeline. Descend 400 feet in a quarter-mile over more limestone steps. Complete this rugged hike by making multiple crossings of the shallow Sabinal River, passing huge boulders, springs, plateau grasslands, and wooded slopes. In spring, you may see the endangered black-capped vireo and golden-cheeked warbler. In October and November the maples display the most awesome fall foliage colors in the state. The park also holds the state's largest Chinkapin oak and bigtooth maple. The park was named for the stand of isolated, uncommon Uvalde bigtooth maples.

Start: East Trail trailhead
Nearest town: Vanderpool
Distance: 3.8-mile loop
Approximate hiking time: 3.5 hours
Difficulty: Strenuous, due to a 500-foot gain over limestone outcrops
Trail surface: Dirt, grass, limestone outcrop
Seasons: September to June
Other trail users: Dog walkers
Canine compatibility: Leashed dogs permitted
Land status: State natural area; Texas Parks & Wildlife Department
Fees and permits: $5 to $6, depending on season, per adult

13 years of age and older. Senior rates available. Or use the State Parks Pass.
Schedule: 8:00 a.m. to 10:00 p.m. daily
Maps: Trail maps are available in the park office. You can also find maps on the Web site www.tpwd .state.tx.us.
Trail contacts: Lost Maples State Natural Area, 37221 Farm Road 187, Vanderpool, TX 78885; (830) 966-3413
Other: Check for restricted park access in December and January, when controlled public hunts are in progress and general access is not permitted.

Finding the trailhead:
Lost Maples State Natural Area is 60 miles west-northwest of San Antonio. From the city take Interstate 10 west to Comfort. Exit and take Highway 27 southwest to Center Point. Go left on Farm Road 480 to Camp Verde, then left on Highway 173. Go right on Farm Road 2828, then go right on Highway 16 to Medina. From Medina, go left on Farm Road 337 to Vanderpool, then right on FM 187. Travel 5.0 miles to Lost Maples State Natural Area and turn left into the natural area. From the overflow parking lot near the park headquarters,

go about 300 yards, following a gravel road, to the East Trail trailhead along the Sabinal River. DeLorme's *Texas Atlas & Gazetteer:* Page 67 J12. GPS: N29° 48' 009" W99° 34' 584"

THE HIKE

The maple trees in this area are growing miles from where they normally grow. The Lost Pines in Bastrop State Park and the dwarf palmettos in Palmetto State Park share the characteristic of being isolated stands of trees located 80 to 200 miles from their natural range. Lost Maples State Natural Area was registered as a National Landmark in 1980.

To start your hike, ford Can Creek using flat rocks on the streambed, then head northwest and upstream. The water in the stream was absolutely clear when I hiked here, possibly due to the unusually heavy rains. There are live oak and cedar trees to the side of the trail, but too far away to furnish shade. Can Creek is on the left (south) and the trail veers slightly to the right and away from the creek. A 25- to 30-foot deep gully leads to the creek.

A trail sign at Can Creek shows directions for the East and West Trails in Lost Maples State Natural Area. East Trail leads to ponds and a strenuous climb up limestone "steps."

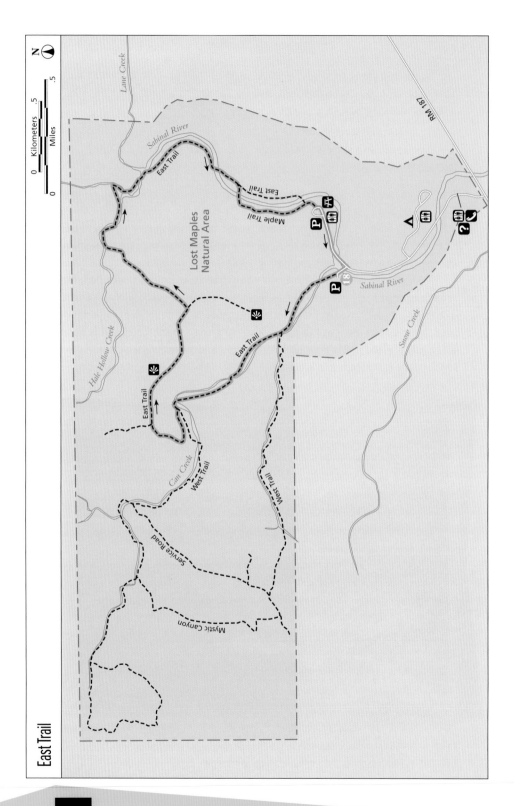

East Trail

The trail branches at a sign located by a limestone ledge in the creek. The left (west) branch leads across the creek to the West Trail. Take the right branch, heading northwest on the east side of the creek. Trees arch over the path furnishing welcome shade. A large limestone outcrop and steep canyon wall are on the right. As the trail narrows it approaches the canyon wall. The creek is on the right and about 25 feet down a slope. Large boulders are scattered on the creek bed, making a very picturesque view. Small fish, about 6 inches long, can be seen swimming in the clear water.

Golden-cheeked warblers, an endangered species, nest in the area east of the creek and, if you're lucky, may be seen during their nesting period in spring. On the west side of the creek are the two largest Chinkapin oaks in the state. These are hard to locate, so if you're interested in seeing them, check with the park ranger.

Head toward the canyon wall, veer to the right, and watch for a marker that shows the elevation as 1,893 feet. The marker is located just a little over 1 mile into the hike. The trail crosses the creek and bends hard left, heading west. There is a large pond and several smaller ones on the left (south), formed by a meadow creating a partial dam across Can Creek. The terrain slopes gently down to the ponds and a picnic area, where you'll find a composting privy.

Wildlife thrives, especially in the valley, but is elusive due to the terrain and size of the park. The most common animals seen are armadillo, white-tailed deer, squirrels, and wild hogs. The wild hogs look menacing with tusks growing out of the sides of their mouths, but generally run for cover when confronted by hikers. Lost Maples State Natural Area is site HOTW 061 on the "Heart of Texas Wildlife Trail," identified by the Texas Parks & Wildlife Department as a prime viewing location.

The canyon walls are ahead and on the right. Start up a steep, rocky section with limestone outcrops forming the trail. These outcrops are called "steps" by the park rangers. This is a long steady climb, gaining about 300 feet in elevation. This is the most strenuous part of the hike and the trail's edge borders the canyon wall, so there are good views into the canyon. Cedars line both sides of the trail. At the top there's a trail branch to Camping Area B.

Red oaks are sometimes called Spanish Oaks.

18

> *Lost Maples State Natural Area is home to the state's largest Chinkapin oak, certified in 2006, and bigtooth maple, certified in 2000.*

Upon reaching the top of the canyon wall, follow the ridgeline. The cedars are short and few, so there's no shade. There are plenty of rocks to sit and rest upon. Once on the ridge you will enjoy one continuous panoramic view of the Sabinal River valley, making the trek up the steps worthwhile. This canyon is deeper than normal for central Texas.

Pass a spur on the right (south) leading to a scenic overlook, but the views from the ridge are better, so there's little need to explore this spur.

Coming down from the ridge is another series of limestone "steps." Some folks call this section "the rock and roll trail" because there are many small rocks across the limestone outcrops, making walking difficult. Pass a sign that points to CAMPGROUND A and a composting privy. Hale Hollow Creek, Lane Creek, and the Sabinal River come together here.

Follow the trail as it turns south and follows the Sabinal. The river will be crossed several times. The crossing is easy since the riverbed is mainly limestone and there are flat rocks to step on. The "Grotto," a large cliff wall overhanging the river, is covered with maidenhair ferns and dripping springs that flow down the walls.

Reach the branch on the right to the short Maple Trail loop. Take the Maple Trail, which goes under a cliff with large boulders in the path and Uvalde bigtooth maple trees furnishing the best fall foliage display in the state. Squeeze through a few tight spots and go up and down several sets of stairs, then head back to the parking area.

MILES AND DIRECTIONS

0.0 Start at the overflow parking area to the East Trail trailhead.

0.2 Arrive at the East Trail trailhead. Continue northwest along the creek.

0.4 Reach a branch at Can Creek. Turn right to stay on the East Trail and continue heading north. The left branch crosses the creek and is the West Trail.

1.0 Cross Can Creek and the large pond created by the partial damming of the creek by a meadow. There is a picnic area and privy here. Follow the trail left (west) and prepare for a steep climb over limestone outcrops. Bear right just as the climb starts. There's little shade and the left edge of the trail has steep dropoffs into the canyon. Be sure you have enough water.

1.3 Reach the top of the climb, which is on the ridgeline looking down into the Sabinal River canyon. Pass a sign on the left pointing to campground b. The terrain at the top of the canyon is flat.

1.9 Pass a branch on the right that goes to a scenic overlook and veer left, heading northeast. The trail gradually descends to steep limestone outcrops. This section has been called the "rock and roll" trail. Small rocks are scattered on the surface of the limestone, and at times making walking precarious.

2.5 Most of the descent back into the valley is completed. Hale Hollow Creek passes near the trail. There's a sign for campground a and a composting privy.

2.7 Follow the trail south. Hale Hollow Creek, Lane Creek, and the Sabinal River converge here. Normally they are all less than 2 feet deep. Cross the river, which puts it to your left (northeast).

3.1 Cross the Sabinal River, heading south.

3.2 Cross the Sabinal River, heading west, then veer left and follow the river heading south. This takes you off the East Trail and leads into the Maple Trail. Follow the Maple Trail up and down some steps and along the canyon walls. The river will be to the east.

3.4 The Maple Trail ends. Go across the main parking area to the overflow parking area.

3.8 End the hike at the overflow parking area.

> 🌿 **Green Tip:**
> *Carry a reusable water container that you fill at the tap.*
> *Bottled water is expensive; lots of petroleum is used to*
> *make the plastic bottles; and they're a disposal nightmare.*

Hill Country State Natural Area: Hermit's Trace

Hermit's Trace in the Hill Country State Natural Area offers strenuous hiking combined with the feeling of being in the wilderness. There are two difficult climbs and descents, made more treacherous by loose rock. Cross several seasonal creeks that are usually dry but may have running water after heavy rains. Signs of flash flooding, a Hill Country phenomenon, can be seen around some of the creek beds, so watch the weather. In October, see roosting monarch butterflies resting during their migration to Mexico.

Start: Near the Equestrian Camp Area at the junction of Trails 3a and 3

Nearest town: Bandera

Distance: 2.3-mile loop

Approximate hiking time: 2.5 hours

Difficulty: Strenuous, due to steep inclines and descents and rough trail surfaces. This is one of the most difficult hikes in the park and not recommended for young children or folks in poor physical condition.

Trail surface: Dirt, loose gravel, and rock

Seasons: September to June

Other trail users: Equestrians, mountain bikers, dog walkers

Canine compatibility: Leashed dogs permitted

Land status: State natural area; Texas Parks & Wildlife Department

Fees and permits: $4 per person or use the State Parks Pass.

Schedule: Daily from dawn to dusk

Maps: USGS Tarpley Pass and Twin Hollows quads. Trail maps are also available in the park office and on the Web site www.tpwd.state.tx.us.

Trail contacts: Hill Country State Natural Area, 10600 Bandera Creek Road, Bandera, TX 78003; (830) 796-4413

Other: Potable water is not available in the park. Bring drinking water. Trails may close during wet conditions. Public hunts are held in December and January; the park is closed to the general public during those events. Check the park calendar for access restrictions, and call the park for specific dates. There is no electricity available in the park. Stay on the designated trails or receive a citation from a park ranger.

Finding the trailhead:

Hill Country State Natural Area is 40 miles northwest of San Antonio. Take Highway 16 northwest to Bandera, then take Highway 173 south, across the Medina River, to Ranch Road 1077. Turn right and drive 10 miles to where the pavement ends and the road becomes gravel. From here follow the signs to the park headquarters area. Obtain a permit and map, then head west on the Park Road to the Equestrian Camp. This is the closest parking. Continue north down the road to the trailhead for Hermit's Trace (Trail 3). Take Trail 3, which is on the left. DeLorme's *Texas Atlas & Gazetteer:* Page 77 A8. GPS: N29° 69' 745" W99° 19' 760"

THE HIKE

Before getting too far into the hike, take the advice a ranger gave about this being a primitive area: "We are a primitive park. If you think you need it, we don't got it—you'll need to bring it!" This honors the request of Louise Merrick when the land was donated to the state after her death, that it ". . . be kept far removed and untouched by modern civilization, where everything is preserved intact, yet put to useful activities."

The area was the Merrick Bar-O-Ranch, a working cattle ranch that began in 1856 and continued operations through the mid-1970s. Since the park opened to the public in 1984, the land has been allowed to revert to its natural condition, and with no electricity it's one of the few parks where stars can be seen at night.

Cross several seasonal creeks that are usually dry but may have running water during or after heavy rains. Continue on Trail 3, heading west and passing the branch where Trail 4a intersects and dead-ends. Make a hard right where Trail 3a merges and start a steep climb, made more difficult by loose rocks. Use caution. This is one of two very strenuous sections on the trail. The top of the hill is a good spot to take in scenic views of the 5,400-acre park, with its rocky hills, flowing springs, oak groves, grasslands, and canyons. From here on the trail is single-track, sometimes rough and overgrown with vegetation.

On the way down, pass connector Trail 3b on the right (east). Trail 3b is an option if this segment of Trail 3a has become too rugged. Otherwise continue on 3a, following the curve and then heading northeast. This portion of 3a heads around a high peak. There's about a 200-foot increase in elevation, going from 1,700 feet to 1,900 feet. During the spring of the year, prickly pear cactus (the state plant), Indian paintbrush, and the colorful and aromatic monarda bush attract and provide nectar for the many species of butterflies in the area. Mountain laurel is scattered through the park and in the spring presents purple and lilac blossoms adding color to the hills.

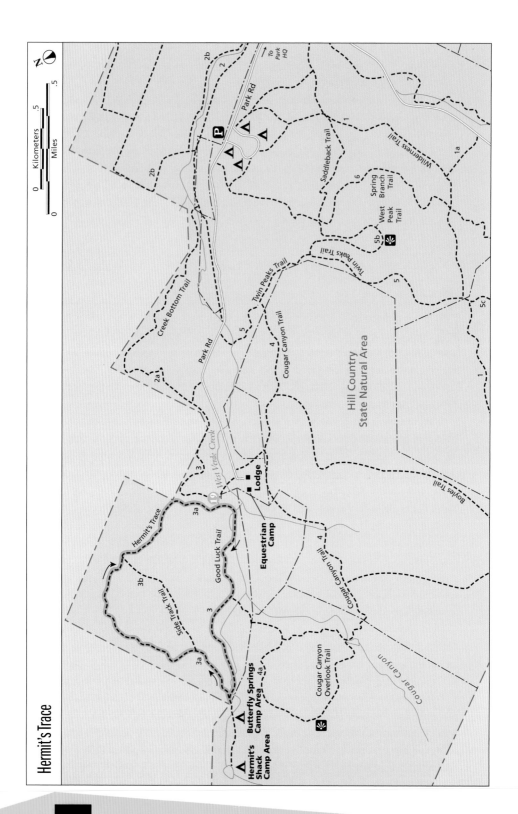

Hermit's Trace

Flash flooding is a common phenomenon of the Hill Country. Creeks that can be waded become raging rivers, leaving trees uprooted and debris scattered. Be aware of the weather while hiking and quickly move to high ground if the water is rising.

Follow the trail to the right, heading southeast, and prepare for another tough climb. Pass the intersection on the right of Trail 3b. From here the trail is still rugged, but the toughest sections are behind you. Follow a curve close to the park boundary and head south to where Trails 3 and 3a join. Turn left and the final stretch will be along the road back to your vehicle.

Wildlife is abundant, particularly along the edges of wooded areas. Take along a bird or mammal guidebook and a set of binoculars to add a dimension to the hike. During October, thousands of monarch butterflies roost in the trees on their migration to Mexico. Listen and watch for white-eyed vireos, (more of a yellow spectacle around their eye than white), summer tanagers, and indigo buntings. Look for white-tailed deer, armadillos, and jackrabbits in the early morning and afternoon.

Always keep an eye out for herds of wild hogs and the venomous western diamondback rattlesnake. The wild hogs, though looking ferocious with tusks growing from their mouths, usually flee when confronted by hikers. For peace of mind when hiking in the Hill Country, it's a good idea to be able to identify the two venomous snakes (western diamondback rattlesnake and water moccasin) from the dozens of nonvenomous snakes that live in the region.

For rugged natural beauty, solitude and some challenging hiking, the trails at Hill Country State Natural Area are difficult to surpass.

MILES AND DIRECTIONS

0.0 Start at Hermit's Trace trailhead.

0.4 Trail 4a intersects and ends on the west side of Trail 3. Continue on Trail 3, heading generally west.

0.8   Trail 3a joins Trail 3; make a hard right turn, heading northeast, and prepare for a rugged steep hike.

0.9   Trail connector 3b intersects and ends at Trail 3a. This is the place to take the less rugged 3b east to rejoin 3a if the trail has become too difficult. If you choose to stay on 3a, continue close to the park boundary, heading northeast.

1.8   Pass connector Trail 3b on the right (south), and continue following Trail 3a.

2.3   Reach the point where Trail 3a joins Trail 3. This is where the Hermit's Trace began. Exit the trail, heading back over the road to the parking lot.

Local Information

For information on Bandera call the Bandera County Convention and Visitors Bureau at (800) 364-3883 or visit the Web site at www.banderacowboycapital.com.

The roots of ranching in Texas were formed at the Spanish missions during the mid-1700s by Indian **vaqueros** *(cowboys) who tended large herds of cattle, goats, and sheep. They marked the stock with branding irons similar to those used in Spain.*

This family is looking for wildlife. Many hikes have trails that follow creeks.

Hill Country State Natural Area: Wilderness and Twin Peaks Trails

Sections of the Wilderness Trail combined with the Twin Peaks Trail is hiking at its best in the Hill Country State Natural Area. A combination of single-track and double-track trails add interest. Go through canyons, up and down rocky hills, past grasslands, and across seasonal creeks to see some of the best scenery in central Texas. The small loop around the Twin Peaks, which are more than 1,800 feet high, has spectacular views. You'll have the opportunity to see riders on horseback, giving you the feeling of stepping back into another era. This hike is not recommended for young children.

Start: Trail 1 trailhead
Nearest town: Bandera
Distance: 3 miles; interconnecting loops
Approximate hiking time: 2 hours
Difficulty: Strenuous, due to steep inclines and descents, rough trail surfaces and, in the summer, heat and humidity
Trail surface: Dirt, sand, and loose rock
Seasons: September to June
Other trail users: Equestrians, mountain bikers, dog walkers
Canine compatibility: Leashed dogs permitted
Land status: State natural area; Texas Parks & Wildlife Department
Fees and permits: $4 per person or use the State Parks Pass.
Schedule: Daily from dawn to dusk

Maps: USGS Tarpley Pass and Twin Hollows quads. Trail maps are also available in the park office and on the Web site www.tpwd.state.tx.us.
Trail contacts: Hill Country State Natural Area, 10600 Bandera Creek Road, Bandera, TX 78003; (830) 796-4413
Other: Potable water is not available in the park. Bring drinking water. Trails may close during wet conditions. Public hunts are held in December and January; the park is closed to the general public during these events. Check the park calendar for access restrictions. Call the park for specific dates. There is no electricity available in the park. Stay on the designated trails, or receive a citation from a park ranger.

Finding the trailhead:
From San Antonio, take Highway 16 northwest to Bandera, then take Highway 173 south, across the Medina River, to Ranch Road 1077. Turn right and drive 10 miles to where the pavement ends and the road becomes gravel. From here. follow the signs to the park headquarters area. Obtain a permit and map,

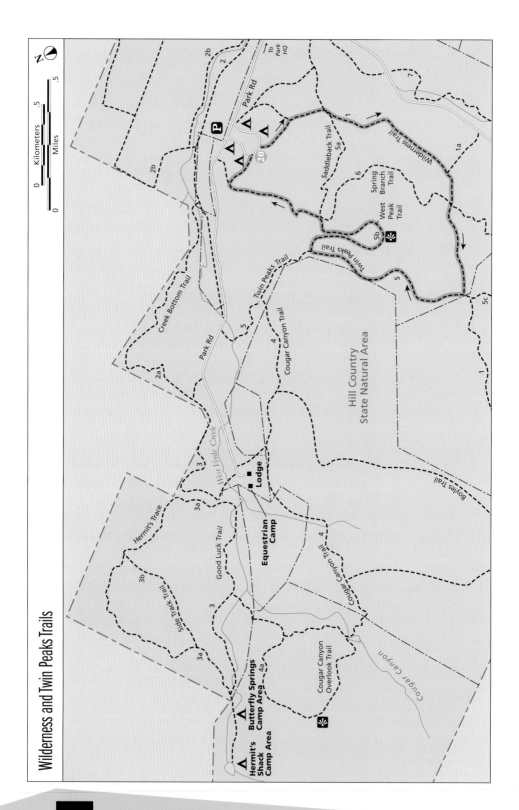

Wilderness and Twin Peaks Trails

then continue on the Park Road, heading west, to trailhead parking, which is at the entrance to camping sites 213–217. The trailhead for Trail 1 is about 0.1 mile from the parking area between campsites 215 and 216. Hill Country State Natural Area is 40 miles northwest of San Antonio. DeLorme's *Texas Atlas & Gazetteer:* Page 77 A8. GPS: N29° 38' 020" W99° 11' 090"

THE HIKE

This is one of the best hikes in the entire Hill Country region because it explores many of the different environments the Hill Country offers, while offering a rigorous, scenic walk.

As you enjoy this area, keep in mind the warning the ranger gave about this being a primitive area: "We are a primitive park. If you think you need it, we don't got it—you'll need to bring it!" This is in keeping with the stipulation from the owners of the Merrick Bar-O-Ranch when they donated the land, that it "... be kept far removed and untouched by modern civilization, where everything is preserved intact, yet put to useful activities."

The route combines sections of Trail 1 (Wilderness Trail, partial loop); Trail 5 (Twin Peaks), and Trail 5b (west peak of the Twin Peaks lollipop).

Head south on Trail 1 (Wilderness Trail), which is double-track, mainly flat, with a few rolling hills. There are four branches with other trails within the first mile, so the hike can be altered to lengthen or decrease the distance. The trails are numbered on the map and there are trail markers at the intersections. Pass these branches and continue on Wilderness Trail, walking beneath the shelter of oaks and cedars. In the fall look for small blue berries, which many birds find tasty, on the cedars. This is also the time to see migrating monarch butterflies fill the skies as they head toward Mexico. In the spring, fields of bluestem grasses and wildflowers decorate the meadows. This is a multiuse trail enjoyed by equestrians, so avoid the manure left by their horses. Look around for dung beetles, unusual in Texas parks, which help clean up the area by feeding on and breeding in the dung.

Swing left, bearing west to a gap. There is a park boundary fence; make a hard right going northeast onto Trail 5, the Twin Peaks Trail. Within a short distance, the trail becomes very steep and rugged, with loose rocks scattered about. This is the most strenuous portion of the hike. The path is mostly single-track and passes to the north of the Twin Peaks. A few wild goats enjoy grazing on these hillsides and jackrabbits take 15-foot hops and jumps to escape anything they think is a predator. Western diamondback rattlesnakes call the Hill Country home and may be seen while hiking. Since they are cold-blooded, they are less active, even hibernating during cold weather. Learn to recognize the venomous snakes (rattlesnakes and water moccasins) from the nonvenomous, so everything that slithers doesn't unnerve you.

Continue heading northeast until Trail 5 branches left and the short Trail 5b loop goes right. Take the loop, making a hard right turn and heading up to the West Peak. This trail is rocky and difficult, causing you to scramble a bit on the climb to the top. Enjoy the 360-degree panorama from 1,870 feet up, as the loop circles the top. This is one of the best spots to appreciate the park's 5,400 acres, with its patchwork of hills, woods, canyons, creeks, and meadows, along with 36 miles of trails. On the way down, there are good views of the valley on the right. The loop ends and leads to markers for Trail 5, which heads downhill toward the campsites. Patches of sotol, a plant resembling yucca, but with the leaves not as rigid, hang over many trails. The sawtooth leaves can leave uncomfortable scratches, so use caution when pushing them aside. Finish the hike back at the trailhead.

An alert doe keeps her eyes on the hikers.

This section of the Hill Country was once part of the Merrick Bar-O-Ranch, a working cattle ranch that began operations in 1856 and prospered through the mid-1970s. The park opened to the public in 1984 and since then has been allowed to revert to its natural condition, including no electricity.

MILES AND DIRECTIONS

0.0 Start at the Wilderness Trail (Trail 1) trailhead. (It's about 0.1 mile from the parking area.)

0.3 Single-track Trail 5a crosses Trail 1 from the west side. Continue straight on Trail 1.

0.8 Trail 1a intersects on the left (south) and dead-ends at Trail 1. Continue forward, veering right.

0.9 Single-track Trail 6 crosses Trail 1. Continue straight on Trail 1.

1.3 The trail branches near a gap at the fence. Turn right (north) onto single-track Trail 5. Prepare for a very steep climb heading north then northeast. The trail has loose rocks scattered on it, making walking precarious.

2.0 Finish the climb and come to a branch. Turn right onto Trail 5a, heading southeast.

2.1 Trail 5b intersects Trail 5a from the right. Turn right and continue on Trail 5b. This steep climb takes you up to Twin Peaks at an elevation of more than 1,800 feet. Follow the loop to the left on Trail 5b. There's an observation point with panoramic views. Complete the loop and then backtrack to the intersection with Trail 5a.

2.4 Trail 5b T branches into Trail 5a. Turn right, heading east.

2.5 Come to a T branch with Trail 6. Turn left onto Trail 6, heading northeast, and begin the easy downhill walk to the campgrounds.

3.0 End the hike at campsites 214 and 215 and backtrack to the parking lot.

Local Information
For information on Bandera, call the Bandera County Convention and Visitors Bureau at (800) 364-3883, or visit the Web site at www.banderacowboycapital.com.

This is a park for river lovers. The Guadalupe River's 4 miles of frontage is awesome. The river's banks are lined with 100–foot-high bald cypress trees and several swirling rapids along steep limestone bluffs. The park is on the Heart of Texas Wildlife Trail–East and is home to several threatened species, including the endangered golden-cheeked warbler. Loop 3 skirts a steep ridge overlooking the Guadalupe River, furnishing a great panorama.

Start: Loop 2 trailhead at the end of the equestrian parking area

Nearest town: Boerne

Distance: 5.6-mile loop

Approximate hiking time: 2.5 hours

Difficulty: Moderate due to steep sections on Loop 3

Trail surface: Dirt path with some loose rocks

Seasons: September to June

Other trail users: Equestrians, mountain bikers, dog walkers

Canine compatibility: Leashed dogs permitted

Land status: State park; Texas Parks & Wildlife Department

Fees and permits: $4 per person

or you can use the State Parks Pass.

Schedule: 8:00 a.m. to 10:00 p.m. daily

Maps: Trail maps are available in the park office. You can also find maps on the Web site www.tpwd .state.tx.us.

Trail contacts: Guadalupe River State Park, 3350 Park Road 31, Spring Branch, TX 78070; (830) 438-2656

Other: Public hunts are held in December and January, during which the park is closed to the general public. Check the park calendar for access restrictions. Call the park for specific dates.

Finding the trailhead:

The park is located 30 miles north of San Antonio. From the city, head north to the intersection of U.S. Highway 281 and Highway 46.

Go west on Highway 46 for 8 miles to Park Road 31. Turn onto PR 31 and follow it for 3 miles to the park entrance. There is a gravel road right across from the park headquarters. Take this to its end and park. The trailhead for Loops 1, 2, and 3 is adjacent to the equestrian parking area. DeLorme's *Texas Atlas & Gazetteer*: Page 68 J6. GPS: N29° 85'242"W98° 50' 143"

THE HIKE

Loops 2 and 3 are combined here to show the best of the open flat land, woodlands, and bluffs overlooking the Guadalupe River. The loops are inter-connecting, which allows simple adjustments to be made during the hike to shorten, lengthen, or change directions. There is a picnic table and several benches at the entrance to the trailhead.

Even though hikers, bikers, and equestrians use this trail, it is underutilized, so there's no lack of solitude. Although this rugged park has limestone terrain typical of the Edwards Plateau, Loop 2 is flat, going through cedar woods and meadows.

A short feeder path leads to the junction of Loop 1 and Loop 2. At the branch continue straight; the right branch is Loop 1, which loops around to intersect Loop 2. After passing through cedar woods with small patches of meadows and some prickly pear cactus (the state plant), come to a Y branch formed by the meeting of the east and west legs of Loop 2. Follow the right leg and head north. Eventually, both legs intersect Loop 3.

Nine-banded armadillos, the state's official small mammal, may be seen in this area during early morning and late afternoon in the fall and winter. Look for armadillo signs, 4-inch oval shallow holes created by their rooting in the dirt. Although armadillos, with their armor plates, look formidable, they are timid animals. They are very slow-moving and if surprised may jump straight up, hoping to startle the intruder.

Small rocks, limestone outcrops, and scrubby bushes can be seen along the edges of Loop 2 in Guadalupe River State Park.

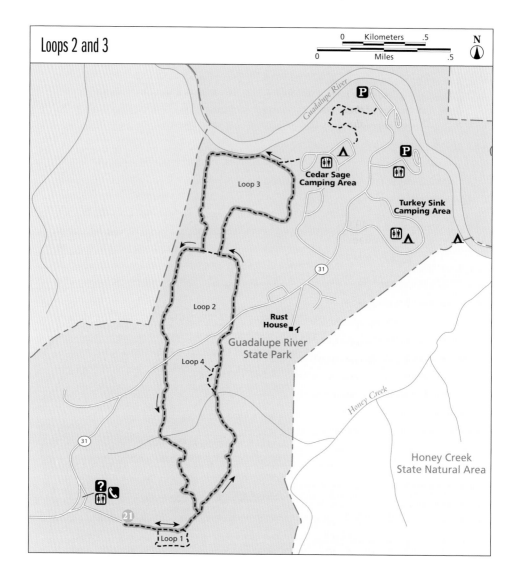

Continue north through live oak and cedar woodlands, interspersed with meadows of King Ranch bluestem grass and a few persimmon, willow, and hackberry trees. There are some low outcrops of black limestone that add to the view.

Park Road 31 crosses the trail so be cautious; on weekends the traffic can be heavy. As you continue north on Loop 2, you'll join Loop 3, which tracks along the

The Guadalupe River was one of the earliest explored rivers in Texas. It was named for Our Lady of Guadalupe by Spanish explorer Alonzo de Leon in 1689.

The cypress is a member of the redwood family and can survive up to 1,200 years, with most living 600 years. Good examples of these trees can be seen along the rivers at Cibolo Nature Center, Guadalupe State Park, and the Medina River Park.

Cedar Sage Camping Area. Campsite 34 is the alternate trailhead for this loop. Following the trail in this area can be confusing. Look for a stock tank and hitching post; the trail continues behind the hitching post. There are rocks on the path, so keep an eye on the ground. The trail skirts the edge of a high bluff overlooking the Guadalupe River. This is the scenic high point of the hike, with the river flowing leisurely around tall limestone cliffs and towering bald cypress trees. Several spurs lead to the edge of the bluff for a better view.

The cliffs have lichens and numerous tiny caves that are home to a variety of wildlife, including the canyon wren, so bring binoculars to add a dimension to the trip. The steep limestone bluffs reflect the river's awesome erosive power. Thanks to a handful of canoeists who lobbied the Texas Legislature in the mid-1970s, this 4-mile stretch of the upper Guadalupe River is now preserved as a state park.

Make a left bend and head south, away from the river. At the T branch with Loop 2, take the right leg heading west. This section of Loop 2 is pretty much a mirror image of the first part of the hike, so head back to the trailhead.

There is an area of virgin cedar woodlands within the park that provides nesting habitat for the endangered golden-cheeked warbler, giving those interested an opportunity to see this rare bird. The 4 miles of river frontage within the park invites swimming after a hike.

The park is adjacent to the Honey Creek State Natural Area. Access to Honey Creek is limited to guided tours given on Saturday, but this is a great opportunity to combine these hikes with a Honey Creek tour. Do the Honey Creek tour first to listen to a Texas master naturalist guide talk about the geology, plants, and animals that exist in the Hill Country.

MILES AND DIRECTIONS

0.0 Start at Loop 2 trailhead adjacent to the parking area. A short connector trail leads to Loop 2.

0.1 Pass the intersection on the right where the west leg of Loop 1 meets the trail.

0.2 Pass the intersection on the right where the east leg of Loop 1 meets the trail.

0.6 Reach the Y branch where Loop 2 connects to itself. Take the right leg, continuing going straight (north).

1.5 The trail crosses Park Road 31. Use caution.

1.9 Loop 3 comes in from the left. Turn right, heading north on Loop 3. Follow Loop 3 as it veers right (east) and then left (north), then passes the Cedar Sage Camping Area, which is east of the trail. The trail is ascending to the top of the bluff.

2.9 Pass campsite 34, which is an alternate trailhead for Loop 3. This is at the top of the bluff and the terrain is flat with scattered rocks.

3.1 An overlook furnishes a sweeping view of the Guadalupe River flowing next to the canyon walls.

3.8 Follow the trail as it bends left and heads south to the T branch with Loop 2. Turn right, heading west onto the Loop 2 Trail. The trail veers left and heads south.

4.3 The trail crosses Park Road 31. Use caution. Continue walking south.

5.0 Reach the branch where Loop 2 connects to itself. Turn right and backtrack to the trailhead.

5.6 End the hike at the trailhead by the parking area.

Local Information

For information about Boerne contact the Boerne Convention & Visitors Bureau, 1407 South Main Street, Boerne, Texas 78006; (888) 842-8080 or (830) 249-7277; www.tex-fest.com/regional/boerne.html.

The Noble Bald Cypress

The majestic 100-foot-tall bald cypress trees bordering many Texas rivers are impressive. They received the name "bald" because they are among the first trees to loose their leaves in fall and the last to bud in spring. The Choctaw Indians used the long fiber-like bark, which is easy to peel off in strips, to make string and rope. The cones are good to use in starting campfires. Their needle-like leaves are soft and appear feathery, while the stout branches are sometimes partly covered by Spanish moss.

The strands of the gray hanging moss, sometimes up to 20 feet long, give the trees an eerie appearance, especially along a riverbank at dusk. The cone-shaped knobby "knees" projecting above the river's surface are from the submerged roots and are a favorite hangout for catfish.

Honey Creek State Natural Area: Honey Creek Interpretive Trail

This guided hike is a must for nature lovers and a flora and fauna primer for all the Hill Country hikes. Take notes as the certified interpretive guide points out and talks about various plants, animals, birds, geology, and history. The diversity of vegetation and limestone formations is a major feature of this area. The trail goes up and down until it reaches the canyon floor of the creek. The clear blue-green water, with the large bald cypress and sycamore trees, provides great photo opportunities. The golden-cheeked warbler, an endangered species, nests here. Entry to Honey Creek State Natural Area is by guided tour only.

Start: Rust House

Nearest town: Boerne

Distance: 2-mile loop

Approximate hiking time: 2 hours

Difficulty: Moderate due to some steep inclines over limestone

Trail surface: Dirt path

Seasons: Year-round

Other trail users: None

Canine compatibility: Dogs not allowed

Land status: State natural area; Texas Parks & Wildlife Department

Fees and permits: $4 per person or you can use the State Parks Pass.

Schedule: Open Saturday for guided tours only. Check with Guadalupe River State Park rangers for dates and times.

Maps: None available for guided tour

Trail contacts: Guadalupe River State Park, 3350 Park Road 31, Spring Branch, TX 78070; (830) 438-2656

Other: This is a guided hike, available by tour only.

Finding the trailhead:
From San Antonio, go north to the intersection of U.S. Highway 281 and Highway 46. Go west on Highway 46 for 8 miles to Park Road 31. Turn onto PR 31 and follow it for 3 miles to the entrance of Guadalupe River State Park. Enter the park and follow PR 31 north to the Honey Creek State Natural Area. The tour assembles at the Rust House. DeLorme's *Texas Atlas & Gazetteer:* Page 68 J6. GPS: N29° 51' 797" W98° 29' 407"

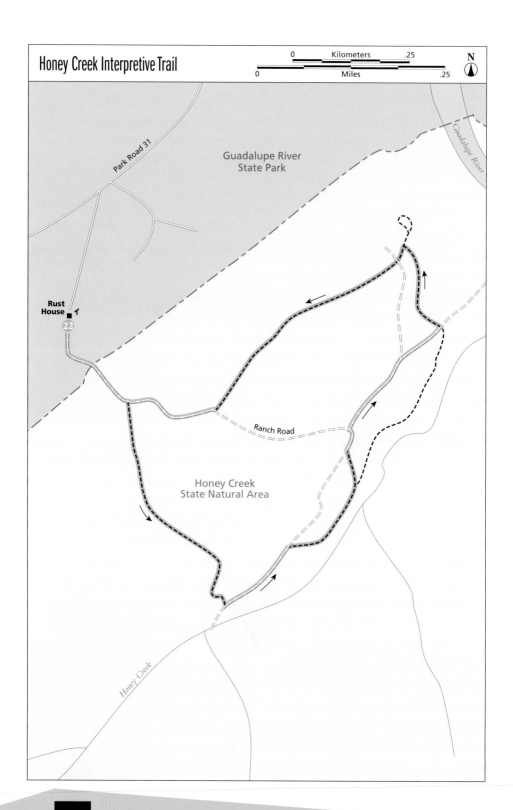

Honey Creek Interpretive Trail

0   Kilometers   .25
0   Miles   .25

N

Park Road 31

Guadalupe River
State Park

Guadalupe River

Rust
House
22

Ranch Road

Honey Creek
State Natural Area

Honey Creek

THE HIKE

History, geology, flora, and fauna are emphasized during this guided tour. Bring a notebook and camera to record information that will later foster curiosity and give added interest to any hike you take. Honey Creek is one of the nesting grounds for the endangered golden-cheeked warbler. The trail is gravel, rock, and dirt.

Meet the guide at the large meadow in front of the Rust House. Entry into Honey Creek is by guided tour only. Leave the meadow and head into the woods. Pass several picnic tables used to display items collected for student classes. Many of the rocks have fossils embedded inside them. The trail leads quickly into heavy forest where Ashe's juniper (cedars), live oak, agarita, and Texas persimmon are predominant. The old-growth Ashe's juniper bark is used by the endangered golden-cheeked warbler to build its nest.

The ball moss hanging on the branches of the live oaks make an eerie site. Going up, down, and around rock formations and over thin soil into the river valley, gives credibility to the fact that this area is one of the most heavily eroded places on earth. Reach an overlook where a small section of the Guadalupe River can be seen. A wooden bench constructed by Eagle Scouts furnishes a good place to enjoy the view.

The clear, green-tinted water of Sugar Creek feeds the lush growth along its edges, including large century-old cypress trees and younger sycamore trees.

As the trail progresses down into the canyon, Honey Creek comes into view. A variety of trees, including cedar elms and the first major occurrence of Spanish oak, pecan, walnut, and Mexican buckeye, form a canopy of shade.

Once in the narrow floodplain of the creek, the path levels. Huge, centuries-old bald cypress and younger sycamore trees cling to and line the creek. Hiking along the cool creek bank allows a glimpse into the clear green-blue water. The color of the water is unusual for Texas creeks. Leopard frogs may be heard near the water.

With the guide, head up the hill from the valley floor. At the top of a knoll watch to the left for some rotting cedar posts and the remnants of a low rock wall meant to keep animals away from crops. The wall was built by an unknown family that farmed here.

To the right is a patch of common mullein, a wild plant with large soft leaves that some Texans call "cowboy toilet paper." There is a steep climb up a set of stone steps. After the stairs, the terrain flattens and the guide will point out a large tree. It is really an odd occurrence that a red oak, a live oak, and a Texas persimmon have all intertwined and almost look like a single multiple-trunked tree. Do not climb on the tree. Follow the guide out of the woods and into a wide meadow that leads to the trailhead.

A group of hikers listen to a guide explain the geology of the karst underground found in the Hill Country.

Beneath the surface of the Edwards Plateau lies the karst habitat, an underground honeycomb of caves, sinkholes, and springs. Various spiders, beetles, and other creatures inhabit this below-ground world and some are unique to this area of Texas.

The Honey Creek area was homesteaded by German immigrants in 1866. Among them, the Doeppenschmidt family became owners of the property that is now the Honey Creek State Natural Area.

Honey Creek is a special place for hikers, with its easy walk, a variety of habitats, and the chance to learn and relax. Try to visit this area in September during the fall migration of thousands of monarch butterflies, the official state insect. Honey Creek State Natural Area adjoins Guadalupe River State Park, which has 6 miles of trails.

Local information

For information about Boerne contact the Boerne Convention & Visitors Bureau, 1407 South Main Street, Boerne, Texas 78006; (888) 842-8080 or (830) 249-7277; www.tex-fest.com/regional/boerne.html.

> *About 15 percent of the land surface in the United States consists of soluble limestone that can be easily dissolved by the weak solution of carbonic acid found in underground water.*

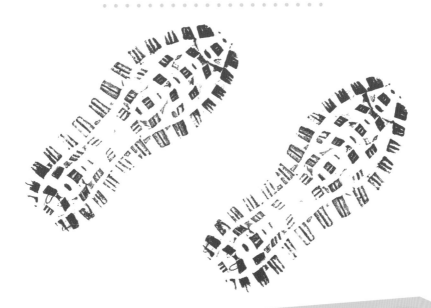

Walking Over the Karst

I was hiking with a friend, who also happened to be a Texas Master Naturalist. We were hiking near the Balcones Canyonlands National Wildlife Refuge, an area of more than 80,000 acres (hike 6) in the Hill Country. This is part of the Edwards Plateau and is one of the largest continuous karst areas in North America.

My companion's specialty was something below the surface, known as the karst. I asked him what in the sam hill a karst is and how does it get there. He started by telling me that karst areas cover about 20 percent of the state. Next, he said I should be familiar with some of the terms. Pointing toward a sinkhole, he informed me that was really a *doline*. Sometime sinkholes can collapse, creating an entrance to an underground cave. Sinkholes are perhaps the most widespread karst feature, while caves are the best known. Next we passed a gully, which had some limestone joints filled with soil—that is a *grike*. There were some rounded blocks of limestone in the gully—these are called *clints*.

Next, he said that many caves have a variety of *speleothems* (rock formations). These structures include stunning examples of *stalactites* (which hang from the ceiling) and *stalagmites* (which stick up from the ground), and other awesome features of karst topography, produced by the deposits of slowly dripping calcium carbonate solutions.

And yes, there are organisms that not only live but thrive in this underground environment. Many of the creatures living in the caves don't have eyes, so some folks call them *eyeless troglodytes* (cave-dwellers). Finally, there was something I could relate to.

A number of species of karst invertebrates are listed as endangered and are found only in Central Texas, like the Helotes mold beetle and the Madla's cave spider. Many of these creatures, like the Batrisodes mold beetle, are difficult to find, due to their size—2 millimeters in length. Texas caves have also yielded important fossils of extinct species, including the Columbian mammoth, dire wolf, flat-headed peccary, ground sloth, scimitar cat, and spectacled bear.

One of the most unusual and very small caves is carved from granite on the top of Enchanted Rock (hike 3). Four karst-created limestone caves are near hiking trails and open to the public: Cascade Caverns and Cave Without a Name (both at Boerne, near hike 23), Inner Space Cavern (Georgetown, near hike 5), and Longhorn Cavern (Burnet, near hikes 1 and 2).

Even deeper below the surface lies another karst formation—the Edwards Aquifer, a reservoir holding billions of gallons of water that supplies drinking water for over one million people in the San Antonio area. The karst topography collects rainwater and routes it underground through streams, caves, and other features, to the aquifer.

My friend then went on about rivers, stating that the San Marcos River (hike 16) receives its water from the San Marcos Springs. The San Marcos and Comal provide water for the Guadalupe River system. He noted that the San Antonio (hikes 27 and 28), Frio, Blanco, and Nueces Rivers originate from karst-fed springs in the Hill Country.

I guess my bewildered look showed I was getting overwhelmed with interesting facts. We had been hiking and talking for a while, yet I still didn't know how a karst is formed. "Enough is enough," I said. "Please tell me how a karst develops before my memory collapses from information overload." He smiled and said, "Sometimes you just resist learning, but I have to have some fun." He then told me that karst is formed out of soluble rocks like limestone, which react with slightly acidic rainwater that drains into joints and fissures, dissolving some of the limestone. This process eventually forms caves and other features, leaving dry stream beds. The water sometimes surfaces as springs, many miles away. I thought, "That's amazingly simple."

Even though I have noticed many sinkholes and been in numerous caves, I never would have imagined this amazing world of karst beneath our feet.

A mother and her young daughter rest and escape the sun under a rock shelter. Several of the rock shelters in the area were used by Native Americans 1,200 years ago.

Cibolo Nature Center: Prairie, Creekside, and Woodlands Trails

Along the Creek Trail, towering bald cypress trees create a canopy for singing birds and darting dragonflies. Look into the clear water of Cibolo Creek to see red-eared slider turtles and catfish. The 4-inch cone-shaped depressions in the sand are from armadillos looking for a meal. Go up a steep bluff to the Woodlands Trail, where the transition zone between the riparian forest, dominated by bald cypress trees, and the live oak savanna is striking. Watch for deer in the early morning and late afternoon. After the hike, look at the castings of the dinosaur tracks near the pavilion. This hike will even hold the interest of young hikers.

Start: Prairie Trail trailhead

Nearest town: Boerne

Distance: 2.2 miles; interconnecting loops

Approximate hiking time: 1.5 hours

Difficulty: Moderate due to the steep uphill path that connects to the Woodlands Trail

Trail surface: Forested dirt path

Seasons: Year-round

Other trail users: Equestrians, dog walkers

Canine compatibility: Leashed dogs permitted

Land status: City park; City of Boerne

Fees and permits: No fees or permits required

Schedule: Trails open 8:00 a.m. to dark daily; park Monday through Friday 9:00 a.m. to 5:00 p.m.; Saturday 9:00 a.m. to 1:00 p.m.

Maps: A map is included in a brochure, available in the visitor center.

Trail contacts: Cibolo Nature Center, 140 City Park Road/P.O. Box 9, Boerne, TX 78006; (830) 249-4616

Finding the trailhead:
Cibolo Nature Center is 30 miles northwest of San Antonio. From the city, take Interstate 10 north about 30 miles to the first Boerne exit, exit 542, which is for Highway 87 northbound. Follow Highway 87 north through the intersection with Highway 46 westbound. Turn right onto River Road (Highway 46 east), which parallels Cibolo Creek. Continue on Highway 46 eastbound for about 1 mile and turn right onto City Park Road. Take City Park Road almost to its end and turn right into the Cibolo Nature Center. The Prairie Trail trailhead is located north of the visitor center. DeLorme's *Texas Atlas & Gazetteer:* Page 68 J5. GPS: N29° 33' 683" W98° 13' 600"

THE HIKE

A pavilion and building close to the trailhead has a large mural-type map of the park painted on the wall, as well as restrooms. Orient yourself then go down a few steps and almost immediately cross a bridge; bear left onto the Prairie Trail to follow the loop counterclockwise. There is a reclaimed pocket prairie to the right containing big bluestem grass, switchgrass, and Indian grass. These "tall grasses" are the type seen in western prairie paintings from the 1900s, where the grass was taller than the belly of a horse. One of the region's most endangered ecosystems, these prairies are part of a major preservation effort at Cibolo to save and replace some of the grasses our grandparents grew up with.

The trail stays close to the creek and several paths lead down to the edge, which is mixed gravel and mud. Large bald cypresses, along with some dogwood and basswood trees, line the shoreline. Many cypress trees are in the water with their "knees" above the surface, causing ripples, swirls, and gurgling as the water rushes by them. This is excellent habitat for catfish; look for them swimming near the trees. Red-eared slider turtles sunning themselves congregate on logs protruding from the water. They are quick to slide into the water when they sense vibrations from your walking.

Pass a stone stairway on the left (east) leading up to the Woodlands Trail. The creek widens a bit here and there are large boulders that you must navigate

These castings were made of tracks from an *Arocanthosaurus*, a 40-foot-long, meat-eating dinosaur. The original tracks were found near Cibolo Nature Center.

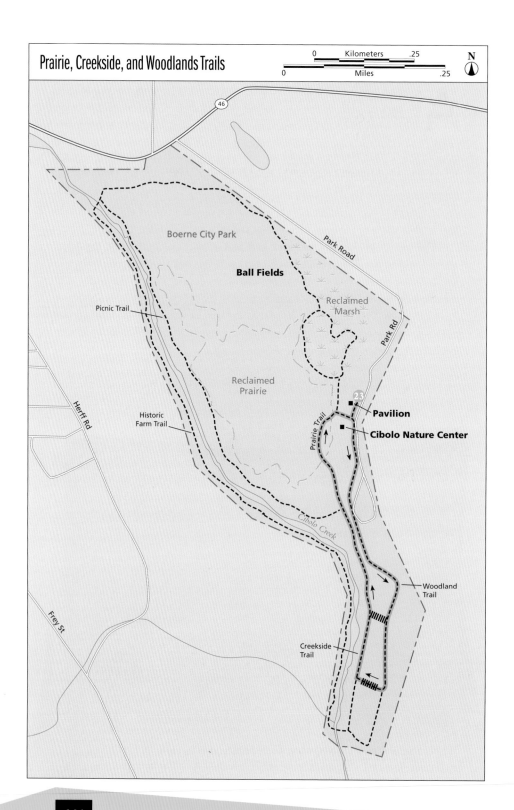

46

Boerne City Park

Ball Fields

Park Road

Reclaimed
Marsh

Picnic Trail

Park Rd

Reclaimed
Prairie

Herff Rd

23

Pavilion

Historic
Farm Trail

Prairie Trail

Cibolo Nature Center

Cibolo Creek

Woodland
Trail

Frey St

Creekside
Trail

around. The creek is nearby on the right, and a bluff is bordering the left. The nature center is noted for the number of animals and birds that are resident here. Seeing them, except for white-tailed deer and squirrels, is difficult because many are active at night. One of the best ways to identify and learn about what animals have been near the trail is to look for signs such as tracks. The tracks of raccoons, skunks, armadillos, and deer are easy to identify and can usually be found near the creek. The armadillo also leaves a nose-print, an oval-shaped depression in the soft earth where they've been rooting for a meal. The footprints of shorebirds may also be seen. This type of "search and identify" activity can even be enjoyed by very young hikers.

At the next stairway turn left, going away from the creek and up the stairs. They are made from stone and are very steep. The stairway acts as the connector to the Woodlands Trail.

The scenery abruptly changes at the top of the hill, from the riparian forest eco-zone that's along the creek to the live oak savanna eco-zone on top of the bluff. This is an excellent example of a sharp line of demarcation between different types of plant life. Ecologists call this transition zone between two different plant communities an ecotone.

Follow the trail on top of the bluff as it heads away from the creek. The trees scattered along the trail are mostly cedar, and prickly pear cactus is abundant. The scenery is totally different from that along the creek. The trail then runs parallel with an electrified wire fence that marks the park boundary. An exotic animal farm is operated on the other side of the fence. Pass a small picnic area and then continue following the trail to the visitor center.

Be sure to check out the 80-foot-long set of castings of dinosaur tracks near the pavilion. The original tracks were found after a major flood in 1997, at the Boerne Lake spillway, preserved in limestone outcrops. It is believed the larger tracks were made by an *Acrocanthosaurus,* a 40-foot-long, three-ton, meat-eating dinosaur that walked on its two hind legs.

MILES AND DIRECTIONS

0.0 Start at the Prairie Trail trailhead, which is located north of the visitor center.

0.1 The trail branches next to a shelter and picnic table. Take the left branch, heading south toward the creek. The right branch is the Cypress Trail. The creek will be on the right.

0.6 Cross a small seasonal stream leading to the creek. The trail narrows and passes between some large rocks. Cibolo Creek is on the right.

0.8   A very steep stone stairway acts as a connector to the Woodlands Trail. At the top of the stairs, turn right onto Woodlands Trail, still going south.

0.9   The Creek Trail intersects on the right (west) and ends at the Woodlands Trail. Bear left, on the Woodlands Trail, and head north.

1.4   Pass the intersection on the left where the Woodlands Trail loop connects to itself, and continue heading north.

1.5   Cross over the intersection with the Cypress Trail. The Park Road is in sight to the right (east). Continue straight (north) toward the pavilion.

2.2   End the hike at the visitor center.

Local Information

For information about Boerne contact the Boerne Convention & Visitors Bureau, 1407 South Main Street, Boerne, Texas 78006; (888) 842-8080 or (830) 249-7277; www.tex-fest.com/regional/boerne.html.

"Ein Prosit"

A toast to the town of Boerne, which has been able to maintain contact with its German heritage for over 150 years. Boerne, a small town of about 7,500 people, is located 22 miles northwest of San Antonio (DeLorme's *Texas Atlas & Gazetteer:* Page 68 J5). It traces its German roots back to 1849 when a few German colonists settled near the Cibolo River and called the place Tusculum. In 1852 the town site was laid out for Boerne. The name was chosen to honor Ludwig Borne, a German poet.

The town states that it has, ". . . the oldest continually organized German band in the world outside of Germany itself." The band has been playing old-country music since the 1860s and the highlight of the year is the *Abendkonzerte,* a series of concerts held each Tuesday in June. The concert takes place on Boerne's main plaza along Hauptstrasse, or Main Street. Strangers to town may be greeted with "Guten tag," which is the German equivalent of a Texas "Howdy."

Toe-tapping polkas and other authentic German music is played, with time being kept by the "oomp pah pah" of the tuba. Children and their parents dance to the tunes. Refreshments are available at the various cafes, coffee shops, bakeries, and pubs. This is an experience to remember, taking you back to when communities were a group of neighbors.

Ein Prosit Boerne; a toast to you.

Government Canyon State Natural Area: Savannah Loop

The Savannah Loop in the front country of Government Canyon State Natural Area is one of the tamer trails in this state natural area. This is a good hike for families. The trail parallels Government Canyon Creek for the first third, and then goes through meadows and woods. A mix of single- and double-track sections adds interest to the hike. Among the animals and birds calling the park home, coyotes, wild hogs, turkeys, venomous and nonvenomous snakes are the most likely to be seen. In October look for monarch butterflies resting in the trees on their migration to Mexico.

Start: Multiuse trailhead at parking lot C

Nearest town: San Antonio

Distance: 2.9-mile lollipop

Approximate hiking time: 1.2 hours

Difficulty: Moderate due to mostly even terrain

Trail surface: Dirt path, a few rocky areas

Seasons: September to June

Other trail users: Mountain bikers, dog walkers, trail runners

Canine compatibility: Leashed dogs permitted, but are restricted to the frontcountry trails

Land status: State natural area; Texas Parks & Wildlife Department

Fees and permits: $6 per person or use the State Parks Pass. A trail permit is required.

Schedule: Open 8:00 a.m. to 6:00 p.m. Friday through Monday (closed Tuesday–Thursday). Access to backcountry trails closes at 4:00 p.m., access to frontcountry trails closes at 5:00 p.m. Protected Habitat Area trails close March 1 to September 1. Laurel Canyon Trail is closed.

Maps: Trail maps are available in the park office. You can also find maps on the Web site www.tpwd .state.tx.us.

Trail contacts: Government Canyon State Natural Area Park, 12861 Galm Road, San Antonio, TX 78254; (210) 688-9055

Other: Before you hike, contact the park for information about trails that may be closed due to inclement weather or poor trail conditions. To reduce the human impact on the natural area, please follow Zero Impact principles of outdoor ethics.

Finding the trailhead:
From Highway Loop 1604 in San Antonio, go 3.5 miles west on Farm Road 471 to Galm Road and turn right (north). Travel for about 1.5 miles to the park entrance at 12861 Galm Road. After checking in at the visitor center, head east on the Natural Area Road to parking lot C. At the back of the lot is

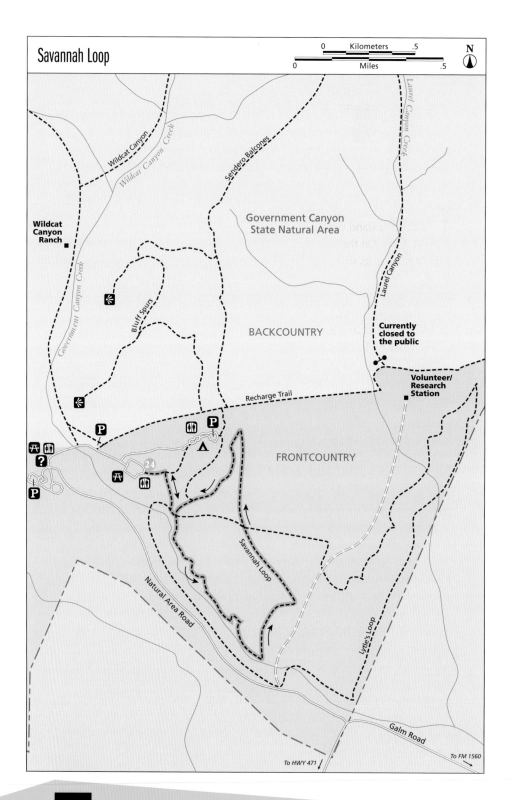

Savannah Loop

0 — Kilometers — .5
0 — Miles — .5

N

Wildcat Canyon

Wildcat Canyon Creek

Sendero Balcones

Laurel Canyon Creek

Wildcat
Canyon
Ranch

Government Canyon
State Natural Area

Government Canyon Creek

Bluff Spurs

Laurel Canyon

BACKCOUNTRY

Currently
closed to
the public

Recharge Trail

Volunteer/
Research
Station

P

24

FRONTCOUNTRY

Savannah Loop

Natural Area Road

Lytle's Loop

Galm Road

To HWY 471

To FM 1560

the multiuse trailhead. Make sure you follow the brown carsonite trail markers with the grass symbol pointing the direction to the start of the Savannah Loop. DeLorme's *Texas Atlas & Gazetteer:* Page 77 B11. GPS: N29° 32' 482" W98° 45' 250"

THE HIKE

Two distinct ecological regions come together in this park. On the northeast is the blackland prairie, containing rolling fields of tall grass and stands of oak trees. On the northwest is the visible dividing line of the uplift of the Edwards Plateau, its valleys and canyons covered with oak and juniper. Geologically, the natural area lies on the Balcones Escarpment, which defines the eastern boundary of the Edwards Plateau. This trail is located in the section of the natural area known as the front country.

Follow the single-track trail south along Government Canyon Creek, which is on the right (east). Cedars and live oak provide a canopy furnishing protection from the Texas sun. Watch along the edges of the trail for horse crippler cactus. These ground-hugging clumps of cactus have hoof-damaging spines, a real hazard to the horses of the cowboys that used to ranch here.

Continue on the flat, gently rolling terrain and look for animal tracks including those of the coyote, which are resident. The amount of wildlife in the area has earned the natural area recognition as site HOTE 085 on the Heart of Texas Wildlife Trail. After passing trail marker 4, head northeast, away from the creek, to a left bend where the trail heads north.

Cowboys call the greater roadrunner the "chaparral cock."

Savannah Loop

The trail widens and in some parts is double-track, but there are a few rocks on the trail to step around. Prickly pear cactus, the state plant, some cedar elms, and mesquite are scattered in the woods. It's possible to see an eastern hognose snake near the trail; they will huff and puff and spread their necks to resemble a cobra. They are harmless and put on an interesting show. Stay on the loop, for venomous western diamondback rattlesnakes also inhabit the park, but really try to avoid people. It's more likely to see squirrels, cottontail rabbits, and wild hogs. The wild hogs usually travel in groups, and with tusks growing out of their mouths present a ferocious image. They take cover if startled by people. In October monarch butterflies may be seen roosting in the oak trees as they held for Mexico.

Nearly three-fourths of the park lies north of the fault line that makes up one of the largest karst preserves in the country. A karst is where groundwater seeps into

A father and daughter descend a trail. Hiking provides an opportunity for family fun and bonding.

an aquifer through sinkholes, caves, and fractures in limestone, in this case filling the Edwards Aquifer and providing homes to many underground-loving creatures.

Near trail marker 9 is a large live oak tree that has recently split, and folks in the area say it used to have a beehive containing tasty honey where the tree branched. Lytle's Loop intersects the Savannah Loop, running to the left (west) and right (east). Continue straight (north) on Savannah Loop and look to the right (east) to see a section of the savanna restoration project. Prescribed (controlled) burns are conducted here to try and restore native flora. Wild turkey and hawks can frequently be seen here. The turkeys are looking for fresh food and the hawks are looking for rodents, which have scarce cover. Patches of mountain laurel grow along this corridor.

The trail narrows a bit and then enters a wooded area that has some open meadows where bluebonnets, the state flower, Indian paintbrush, and other wildflowers can be seen from March through May. Birds like this area and, depending on the time of year, cardinals, painted buntings, and summer tanagers may be seen.

The trail makes a sharp turn to the left and the direction abruptly changes from north to southwest. The loop ends at trail marker 1, where you backtrack on the feeder trail to the parking lot.

MILES AND DIRECTIONS

0.0 Start at the multiuse trailhead at parking lot C. Follow the feeder trail for 0.3 mile (head east for 500 feet, then south for about 750 feet, then southeast for 200 feet) until you arrive at the start of the Savannah Loop.

0.3 Reach the Savannah Loop and follow it counterclockwise.

0.8 Head south to reach trail marker 4.

1.2 Travel northeast to reach trail marker 7.

1.6 Travel north to reach trail marker 9; the trail changes to a wider path. Reach the intersection of Lytle's Loop, which crosses on the left and right. Continue straight (north) on Savannah Loop.

2.4 Continue north to where the trail makes a sharp turn southwest. End the loop at trail marker 1 and backtrack on the feeder trail.

2.9 After completing the Savannah Loop, retrace your steps to parking lot C.

Government Canyon State Natural Area: Bluff Spurs

Imagine an area ten times as large as New York City's Central Park with 36 miles of trails . . . that's Government Canyon State Natural Area. Geology buffs will find the Edwards Plateau limestone intriguing and wonder just how deep the karst underground is. Walk on the geological fault that separates the Edwards Plateau and the blackland prairie ecosystem. Watch for wild hogs, nonvenomous and venomous snakes, and the endangered golden-cheeked warbler. Scramble down steep limestone outcrops, misleadingly called steps. View 80-foot canyon walls cut by Government Creek through layers of limestone as the trail leads through meadows, woods, valleys, and to high overlooks.

Start: Recharge Trail at parking lot D

Nearest town: San Antonio

Distance: 3.5-mile loop, including the feeder trail from the trailhead

Approximate hiking time: 2 hours

Difficulty: Moderate due to several challenging and rocky uphill portions entering the Balcones Escarpment. The last portion of the hike heads downhill on limestone-outcrop stairs.

Trail surface: Dirt, rocky limestone outcrop

Seasons: September to June

Other trail users: None

Canine compatibility: Dogs are not permitted anywhere in the backcountry.

Land status: State natural area, Texas Parks & Wildlife Department

Fees and permits: $6 per person or use the State Parks Pass. Trail permits are required.

Schedule: Open 8:00 a.m. to 6:00 p.m. Friday through Monday (closed Tuesday to Thursday). Access to backcountry trails closes at 4:00 p.m., access to frontcountry trails closes at 5:00 p.m. Protected Habitat Area trails close March 1 to September 1. Laurel Canyon Trail is closed.

Maps: Trail maps are available in the park office. You can also find maps on the Web site www.tpwd .state.tx.us.

Trail contacts: Government Canyon State Natural Area Park, 12861 Galm Road, San Antonio, TX 78254; (210) 688-9055

Other: Before you hike, contact the park for information about trails that may be closed due to inclement weather or poor trail conditions. To reduce the human impact on the natural area, please follow the Zero Impact principles of outdoor ethics.

Finding the trailhead:
From Highway Loop 1604 in San Antonio, go 3.5 miles west on Farm Road 471 to Galm Road and turn right (north). Travel for about 1.5 miles to the park entrance at 12861 Galm Road. Proceed to the park headquarters; the trailhead is to the east in parking lot D. DeLorme's *Texas Atlas & Gazetteer:* Page 77 B11. GPS (park headquarters): N29° 55' 276" W98° 74' 429"

THE HIKE

This hike is in the area of the park known as the backcountry. Getting to the trailhead requires walking through an open meadow on Recharge Trail, which is on the fault that separates the blackland prairie to the south and the Edwards Plateau to the north.

Once on the Bluff Spurs Trail, start climbing uphill on the single-track rocky track. Be careful if it has recently rained, for the rocks can be slippery. Ashe's juniper, mountain laurel, and cedar elm woods form a welcome sun-shielding canopy overhead.

Those folks interested in geology will have a field day studying the exposed Edwards limestone. There are also excellent examples of karst limestone. The karst habitat lies beneath the surface of the plateau and is a honeycomb of caves, limestone channels that carry water, sinkholes, and springs. Sinkholes, the thumbprint of a karst, are created when a cave erodes and enlarges upward to the surface. Various spiders, beetles, and other creatures inhabit this below-ground world, with some being found only in this area of Texas.

Cross over some dry creek beds and look for old-growth cedar trees. These are ideal habitat for the endangered golden-cheeked warbler and it's possible to see them during nesting season.

Reach the Bluff Spurs signpost 2, where the trail branches, and take the left branch heading southwest toward the South Bluff Spurs Overlook. It's a short walk, less than 0.5 mile, and passes through a meadow with the terrain fairly level until the overlook area is reached. Just before the overlook, the trail is single-track, very rocky, and has a few steep steps that lead down. The view is impressive, with hikers able to see the visitor center buildings, a couple of windmills (from the days when this was a ranch), and the Joe Johnston Trail directly below. The trail dead-ends here among prickly pear cactus, the state plant, sotol, and large rocks that furnish a place to sit and rest.

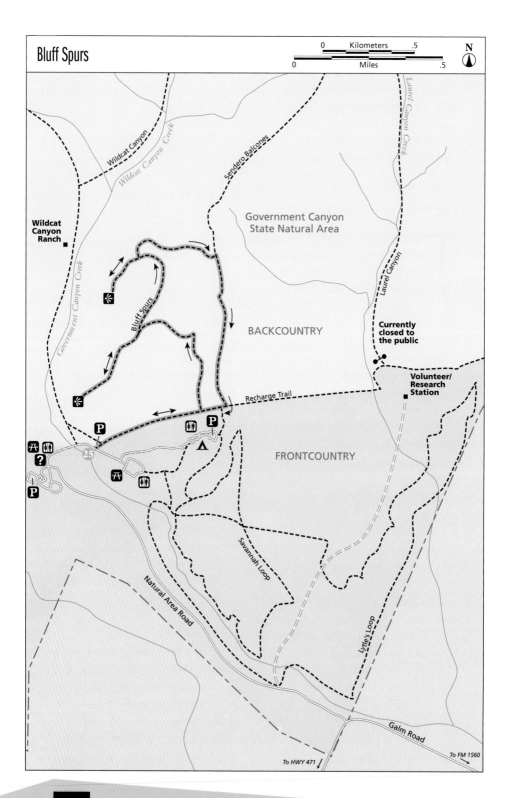

Bluff Spurs

0 Kilometers .5
0 Miles .5

N

Wildcat Canyon

Wildcat Canyon Creek

Laurel Canyon Creek

Sendero Balcones

Government Canyon
State Natural Area

Wildcat
Canyon
Ranch

Government Canyon Creek

Bluff Spurs

Laurel Canyon

BACKCOUNTRY

Currently
closed to
the public

Volunteer/
Research
Station

Recharge Trail

FRONTCOUNTRY

25

Savannah Loop

Natural Area Road

Lytle's Loop

Galm Road

To HWY 471

To FM 1560

Many mammals call the canyon home, among them coyote, Virginia opossum, skunk, raccoon, bobcat, and white-tailed deer. Actually seeing them can be difficult, but add another dimension to the hike by taking along a field guide to animal tracks and trying to identify the various tracks around the trails. Seeing the print left by a bobcat's paw might give the hike a feel of backcountry adventure.

Backtrack to the Bluff Spurs intersection and continue straight (north). Go about 0.3 mile, following a gentle left turn, to the Bluff Spurs signpost 4. The trail is single-track, going through wooded areas that furnish some shade and leading to the North Bluff Spurs Overlook, which is identified by North Spur signpost 2. Looking north from the overlook it is possible to see residential development, while to the west are hills.

Backtrack a short distance to where you turned off to get to the overlook and follow the trail until it dead-ends by intersecting with the Sendero Balcones Trail.

Trails in Government Canyon State Natural Area wander through limestone and scrub cedar and offer great vistas of the surrounding Hill Country.

This is an interesting section affectionately referred to by the park rangers as the "hog wallow," due to the large number of wild hogs usually seen here. This last section of the route, on Sendero Balcones Trail, is a very steep downhill limestone staircase (not real stairs, but outcroppings of limestone rocks), which makes it scenic but strenuous. Fortunately there's a bench to rest on about halfway down. Continue to the Recharge Trail and backtrack to the parking lot.

MILES AND DIRECTIONS

0.0 To get to the Bluff Spurs trailhead start at parking lot D, on the Recharge Trail, and head east.

0.3 Reach the branch with the connector to Bluff Spurs Trail. Turn left, heading north to walk the loop clockwise.

0.9 Reach the Bluff Spurs Trail at signpost 2. Turn left and head southwest (GPS: N29° 33' 063" W98° 45' 199").

1.3 Reach the South Bluff Spurs Overlook. This is an out-and-back section of the trail. Backtrack to signpost 2.

1.7 Reach signpost 2 and pass the connector trail on the right (east). Stay on the Bluff Spurs Trail heading northeast.

2.0 Reach North Spur signpost 2, where the trail branches. Turn left, heading southwest, going to the North Bluff Spurs Overlook.

2.2 Reach the overlook. The trail is single-track just before the overlook. This is another out-and-back section. Backtrack to signpost 2.

2.4 The trail branches. Take the left branch, heading northeast.

2.7 The Bluff Spurs Trail intersects and dead-ends at the Sendero Balcones Trail. Turn right, heading south. The last half of this trail is very steep downhill on limestone.

2.8 Reach the intersection with the Recharge Trail. Turn right (west) and follow the Recharge Trail to the parking lot D.

3.2 End the hike back at parking lot D.

The horned lizard is the Texas state reptile. The armadillo is the official state small mammal.

Wild Hogs

Walking up on a bunch of wild (feral) hogs that are rooting around the ground, snorting and eating, can be startling. This experience is becoming more common on some of the trails in Central Texas. It's possible to see a few stragglers or even a herd of twenty or more. Typically, the females (sows) travel in family groups called *sounders,* while the males (boars) travel alone. The animals can be intimidating—up to 3 feet tall and 5 feet long with two upper and two lower tusks growing from the sides of their mouths. They can weigh up to 300 pounds, but 130 is more typical. They have been called European boars, wild boars, razorbacks, pineywoods rooters, wood hogs, and other names reserved for private conversations.

While hiking, watch for signs of hogs—plowed-up ground where they searched for food and wallows, wet muddy places where they cool off. I have heard stories that wild hog boars are the poor man's grizzly bear and that they are some kind of super-armored beast that is almost impossible to destroy. These stories were probably spread by folks who had never hunted a grizzly bear.

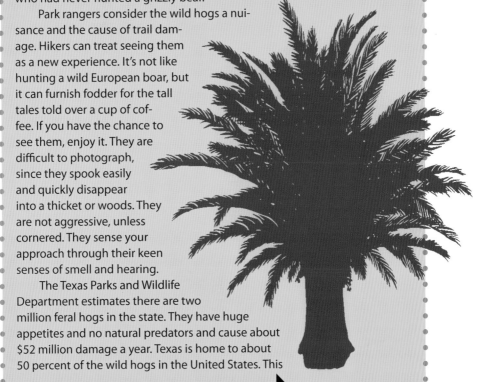

Park rangers consider the wild hogs a nuisance and the cause of trail damage. Hikers can treat seeing them as a new experience. It's not like hunting a wild European boar, but it can furnish fodder for the tall tales told over a cup of coffee. If you have the chance to see them, enjoy it. They are difficult to photograph, since they spook easily and quickly disappear into a thicket or woods. They are not aggressive, unless cornered. They sense your approach through their keen senses of smell and hearing.

The Texas Parks and Wildlife Department estimates there are two million feral hogs in the state. They have huge appetites and no natural predators and cause about $52 million damage a year. Texas is home to about 50 percent of the wild hogs in the United States. This

▶

population includes domestic hogs gone wild, European boars, and crosses between the two. This mixture was initiated in the 1930s when Texas ranchers released wild Eurasian boars for hunting. One sow can generate more than 1,000 offspring in five years. Some folks at the Texas Cooperative Extension Service said to think of a feral hog as a four-legged fire ant and that we are not going to eradicate them, but hope to reduce their population.

Trails where wild hogs have been seen include: Beebrush Loop (hike 2); Wolf Mountain (hike 4); Flag Pond (hike 13); East Trail (hike 18); Hermit's Trace (hike 19), and Bluff Spurs (hike 25). Ask a ranger prior to your hike if wild hogs are present and the most likely locations to encounter them.

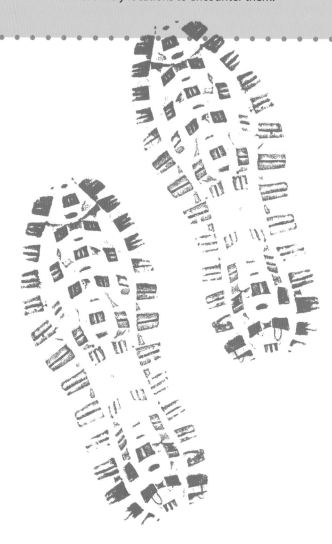

San Antonio Parks and Recreation: McAllister Park Loop

See white-tailed deer on the fringes of the woodlands while hearing songbirds hid-den in the trees. Linger by a creek or in the cool shade of huge live oaks that border the trail. Skirt the edges of baseball diamonds and soccer fields, and strangely enough, at times, you'll seem almost alone in this 986-acre park, San Antonio's largest and most popular park. Although there are 15 miles of dirt trails, including those for mountain biking and many paths made by "trail blazers," the authorized hiking trail is asphalt, 3 miles long, and wheelchair accessible.

Start: Trailhead adjacent to pavil-ion and first parking area
Nearest town: San Antonio
Distance: 2.7-mile loop
Approximate hiking time: 1.5 hours
Difficulty: Easy due to flat, wide paved surface
Trail surface: Asphalt
Seasons: Year-round
Other trail users: Dog walkers, bikers
Canine compatibility: Leashed dogs permitted

Land status: City park; San Antonio Parks and Recreation Department
Fees and permits: No fees or permits required
Schedule: 6:00 a.m. to 10:00 p.m.
Maps: None are available at the park, but maps are on the Web site www.sanantonio.gov/sapar/ mcallistertrail.asp.
Trail contacts: McAllister Park, 13102 Jones–Maltsberger Road, San Antonio, TX 78247; (210) 207-8480

Finding the trailhead:
In San Antonio, from Interstate Loop 410, drive 3.2 miles on U.S. Highway 281 to Bitters Road. Turn east onto Bitters Road to the junction with Starcrest, then continue on Starcrest to Jones–Maltsberger Road. Turn left on Jones–Maltsberger and pro-ceed 1 mile to the park entrance on the right, at 13102 Jones–Maltsberger. Start from the trail-head adjacent to the first parking area. This is only one of many entries onto the trails from various park locations. DeLorme's *Texas Atlas & Gazetteer:* Page 157 F9; page 77 A12. GPS: N29° 32' 849" W98° 27' 121"

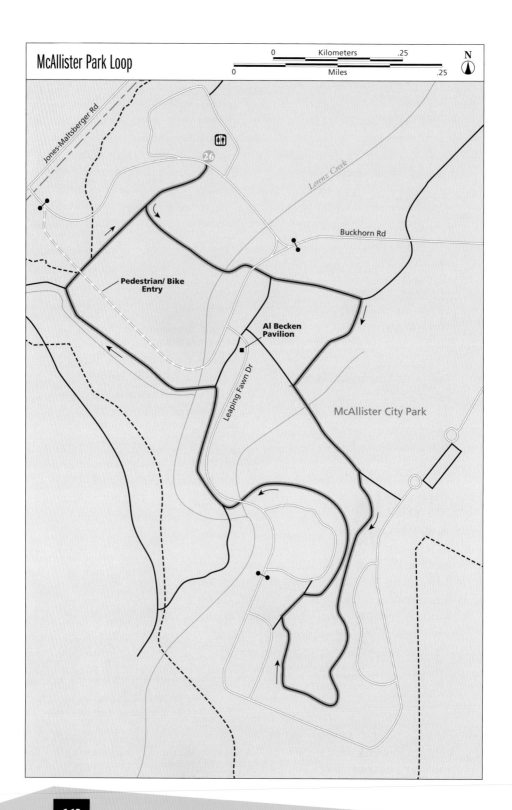

McAllister Park Loop

Jones-Maltsberger Rd

Lorenz Creek

26

Buckhorn Rd

Pedestrian/ Bike Entry

Al Becken Pavilion

Leaping Fawn Dr

McAllister City Park

THE HIKE

The trail, even though closely bordered by trees, is wide enough to accommodate walkers, joggers, and cyclists. The baseball diamonds and soccer fields on the east side of the park are sometimes visible, but generally go unnoticed. There are several well-marked road crossings, so use care.

Start out to the southwest on the asphalt trail. In about 0.5 mile pass the Al Becken Pavilion on the left. Cross Lorenz Creek and pass under huge live oaks bordering the trail that create a sense of a pristine area. Almost immediately cross a park road.

The park, created in 1968, was originally called Northeast Preserve. It was renamed in 1974 to honor former San Antonio mayor Walter W. McAllister. Portions of the park were developed on a floodplain to help protect the San Antonio International Airport. A dam has been built to help control the water level in the Upper Salado Creek watershed. Considering the nearness of the airport, the park has areas that seem pristine, and the woods muffle much of the noise from the air traffic.

Although McAllister Park is within the city limits of San Antonio, the trail leads by swamps and large live oak trees that give the park a pristine appearance.

> *The Edwards Aquifer is the sole source of drinking water for San Antonio and many other communities in this region.*

Many paths made by overzealous "explorers" crisscross the official 3-mile asphalt trail. Stay on the asphalt trail because some areas in the park are ecologically sensitive. There is no official trailhead, but there are entry spots from numerous parking areas. It is one of the few parks where this capability exists and allows the 3-mile hike to be shortened with no worry about getting disoriented. The entire trail is wheelchair and stroller accessible.

Huge live oak trees can be seen near drainage waterways in the lower areas. The trees achieved their unusual size because they could not be cut as they were in a floodplain. They have created a large wooded area that is home to white-tailed deer, rabbits, squirrels, and other wildlife. The largest concentration of birds, squirrels, and other animals is near the picnic area, where they scavenge the crumbs dropped by picnickers. The upland area of the park had been used as a dairy farm and as a result there are a few cedar trees and some mesquite overgrowth. The San Antonio Road Runners and Harmony Hills Optimist Club have helped construct several of the trails in the park.

This park is an anomaly. It's in a major city, sits on a floodplain, adjoins a major airport, and has baseball diamonds, soccer fields, and a police substation, yet McAllister Park has become a favorite hiking destination for folks living in San Antonio. They appreciate its convenient location, the easy hiking trail that is suitable for all ages, the shaded and sometimes almost secluded areas, and the opportunity to relax while watching white-tailed deer and listening to the many species of birds singing near the trail's edge. It's a great getaway that can be utilized even during a lunch break.

MILES AND DIRECTIONS

0.0 Start at the trailhead by the parking lot and head southwest, following the paved trail in a counterclockwise direction.

0.2 Cross the pedestrian entry walk. Continue straight.

0.3 Make a hard left turn heading southeast. Continue straight with a few back-and-forth curves.

0.6 Pass by the Al Becken Pavilion and another trailhead. At the trail intersection turn right, heading south.

0.8 Bend left, heading southeast. A park road is on the left.

1.0 Bend left heading east, cross Lorenz Creek and immediately cross Leaping Fawn Drive. Be cautious of automobile traffic. Bend right (southeast).

1.2 Curve right (south). Pass a trail on the right; stay to the left, heading southwest.

1.3 Bend left (south).

1.4 Bend hard left heading southeast. Continue straight encountering a few back-and-forth curves.

1.5 Take another hard left, this time toward the north-northeast.

1.8 A trail comes in from the right. Continue straight, which is the left branch, heading north-northwest.

2.0 Turn right, heading northeast.

2.2 Turn left (west).

2.4 Pass a trail on the left. Continue straight and then cross Buckhorn Road. Be cautious of automobile traffic.

2.6 Rejoin the original trail at the Y, turning right and retracing your steps toward the trailhead.

2.7 End the hike back at the parking lot.

🌿🌰 Green Tip:
If you're toting food, leave the packaging at home. Repack your provisions in ziplock bags that you can reuse and that can double as garbage bags on the way out of the woods.

Mustang Grapes—A Texan Tradition

If you're a native Texan, mustang grape jelly is likely part of your life and growing up. It's a tradition with many families, who harvest the grapes every summer. Those who have had jelly on warm, fresh-baked bread, have fond memories.

Mustang grapes were plentiful when Spanish missionaries arrived in Texas in the 1700s. They first used them for food and later made sacramental wine from them. European settlers who came to Texas in the mid-1800s applied their winemaking skills to the grapes as well. Seems they didn't bother with jelly until later.

This native grape grows over much of central and other sections of Texas. Its name, like the wild mustangs that once roamed the state, has a bit of romance to it. It is very hardy and has managed to survive the extremes of Texas weather. Growing wild, it climbs trees, covers fence rows, bushes, and any place it can get a hold—some of the runners are 100-feet long. Kids even use the larger vines to swing on. These small grapes can be seen all over the landscape while you're hiking various trails. Folks have tried to kill them, but it's a lot easier to accept them and enjoy their bounty.

If you're interested in making use of them, mid-July is the time to start looking for the ripe grapes. They are reaching their prime, and their color has gone from pale green to reddish, and finally to dark purple. If you're going to pick some, watch your step when you're gathering them, as there's always the chance that a diamondback rattler could be in the grape patch.

The ripe grapes are extremely tart and nearly inedible, but they make great jelly. The jelly has practically no resemblance to concord grape jelly. Be careful not to confuse the grapes with similar but inedible fruits. This staple from the old days is one of the essential items for preserving Texas's culinary heritage.

People aren't the only ones who enjoy the grapes. Birds and hungry raccoons search the uppermost branches for the fruit, while deer, coyotes, and squirrels find their meals on the lower branches. These critters savor the mustang grape straight from the vine.

San Antonio Parks and Recreation: Paseo del Rio

The Paseo del Rio, also known as the RiverWalk, utilizes both sides of the historic San Antonio River in downtown San Antonio. This is one of the few places in the world where there is a 6.1-mile hike, 20 feet below street level, over concrete, flagstone, and cobblestone surfaces. Always a spot to sit and rest, have lunch, or just chat. The RiverWalk is multifaceted, serene, and parklike in some areas, while others are full of activity, offering access to European-style sidewalk cafes, nightclubs, and the history and bustle of the city. This is a really different hike, suitable for all ages. While I recommend my favorite route, this is easily a "make your own" hike. Check the map to choose your entrance from the five that are available.

Start: Near the Alamo in downtown San Antonio

Nearest town: San Antonio

Distance: Up to 6.1 miles; loop with portions of out-and-back

Approximate hiking time: 2.5 hours (for 6.1-mile hike)

Difficulty: Easy due to paved flat terrain

Trail surface: Asphalt, concrete

Seasons: Year-round

Other trail users: Dog walkers

Canine compatibility: Leashed dogs permitted

Land status: City park; San Antonio Parks and Recreation Department

Fees and permits: No fees or permits required

Schedule: Open 24 hours a day. Paths are lighted.

Maps: A map is available from the Web site www.riverwalkmap.com.

Trail contacts: San Antonio Park Police, 600 Hemisfair Plaza Way, San Antonio, TX 78205; (210) 207-8590

Finding the trailhead:
From downtown San Antonio, park near the Alamo, 1301 West Travis Street. The Alamo parking lot at 118 Broadway Street is convenient and less than a block north of the Alamo. The parking fee is $8 per day. DeLorme's *Texas Atlas & Gazetteer:* Page 77 B12. GPS: N29° 25' 539" W98° 29' 173"

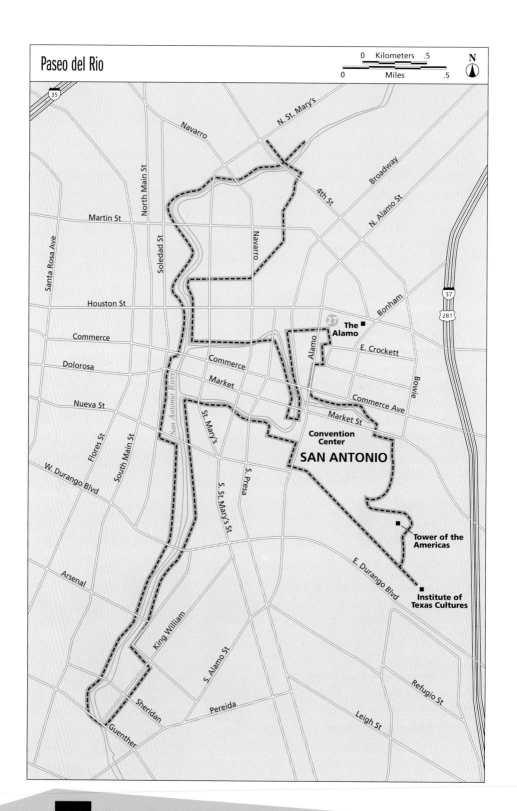

Paseo del Rio

0 Kilometers .5
0 Miles .5

N

Navarro

N. St. Mary's

Broadway

North Main St

Martin St

Soledad St

Navarro

4th St

N. Alamo St

Santa Rosa Ave

Houston St

Bonham

37
281

Commerce

27 The
Alamo

E. Crockett

Dolorosa

Commerce

Alamo

Bowie

Market

Commerce Ave

Nueva St

St. Mary's

Market St

San Antonio River

Flores St

South Main St

S. St. Mary's St

S. Presa

Convention
Center

SAN ANTONIO

W. Durango Blvd

Tower of the
Americas

Arsenal

E. Durango Blvd

Institute of
Texas Cultures

King William

S. Alamo St

Refugio St

Sheridan

Pereida

Leigh St

Guenther

THE HIKE

The starting and ending point for the RiverWalk is your choice, since there are five entrances. This is one of the few hikes in this guide that can be tailored to specific desires and needs, a kind of "make your own" trek. It offers something to people wanting a 6-mile workout (on the out-and-back version of the hike) and to those wanting to walk a few blocks. The young, the old, those needing a stroller, a walker, or wheelchair access can enjoy this walk. There's no need to worry about safety or making a wrong turn and getting lost. In addition, history buffs and those folks interested in Victorian homes can have a field day.

The Paseo del Rio winds through the middle of the business district in downtown San Antonio. The Municipal Auditorium and Conference Center are on the north end, and the King William historic district with its nineteenth-century mansions is on the south end.

One of my favorites hikes on the RiverWalk starts at The Alamo. Go west across Alamo Plaza and cross Alamo Street. The San Antonio Visitor Center is located in the building on the north corner. Stop here to pick up information about the RiverWalk and San Antonio. Turn right after leaving the Visitor Center, and go down a flight of steps to the Hyatt Hotel Atrium Shops. Continue through the shops to the exit that goes to the RiverWalk.

A hiker relaxes on a bench made from the trunk of a pine tree with the San Antonio River behind him.

Turn right after leaving the Atrium Shops; the San Antonio River will be on the left (south). The walk is paved with flagstone and brick. The area is busy since there are coffee shops, restaurants, and pubs forming a wall to the right. The vegetation is tropical and lush. Some type of flower is in bloom nearly all year. The trees (by Texas standards) are gigantic, some being more than 10 feet in circumference, and provide welcome shade. Ducks swim in the river, and pigeons pick up crumbs from the path.

Pass under Houston Street. There is an elevator (that can hold a wheelchair) and stairs going up to street level. These are on the right. Bear left, heading west. The river is on the left and the path borders its bank. There is no way to stray off the path, unless it is to investigate one of the stores or eateries and this presents a great temptation. Pass a plaque on the right that locates the home of Ferdinand Ludwig Herff (1820–1912) built in the nineteenth century. Continue enjoying the tropical scenery and aromas from the restaurants.

Looking up, you can see Navarro Street, which crosses overhead. Hikers, shoppers, and diners all share the space on each side of the river. An artificial waterfall on the right tumbles down to the walk level and then flows into the San Antonio River through sluices cut across the path. The arched stone pedestrian bridge on the left crosses to the south side of the river. The arched stone bridges were the pride of architect Robert Hugman, the "father" of the RiverWalk.

Reach the floodgates that control water from the main branch of the San Antonio River. A plaque states that the Works Project Administration worked on this flood control system between 1938 and 1940. Go up the stairs and at the top,

Historical Items

While sitting at a table or walking along the river, here are a few bits of historical information that can add another dimension to your River Walk outing.
- In 1536 Alvar Núñez Cabeza de Vaca, a shipwrecked captive of the local Native Americans, became friendly with them and was taken to the interior of Texas, where he saw and described the river in his notes. That was over 570 years ago.
- On June 13, 1691, Domingo Teran de los Rios, first governor of the new Province of Texas, accompanied Father Damian Massanet on his return trip to east Texas. They camped at a ranch on a stream called Yanaguana. Someone suggested that since they were there on Saint Anthony's day, the river be renamed to honor the saint. So, we now have the San Antonio River.
- In 1736 construction began on the first bridge to cross the San Antonio River, connecting the Presidio with Mission San Antonio. It was at the site of the present Commerce Street bridge.

turn left (south) and at the bottom turn left (east) to reach the RiverWalk on the south side of the river.

Continue to backtrack along the river's edge to the trail starting point at the Alamo. Time allowing, a visit to the Alamo adds another dimension to the walk. Now pick another entry point to the RiverWalk and create your own favorite hike.

MILES AND DIRECTIONS

0.0 Start at the front entrance of the Alamo.

0.1 Head east across Alamo Plaza continue straight, crossing Alamo Street. Go down the steps and enter the Hyatt Hotel Atrium Shops. Continue through the shops to the exit onto the RiverWalk.

0.2 Turn right (north), the San Antonio River will be on the left.

0.25 Pass under Houston Street. An elevator (can hold wheelchair) and a stairway to the street is on the right. Bear left, continuing west and following the north side of the river.

0.3 Pass by the Ferdinand Ludwig Herff (1820–1912) home, which is on the right. Then continue on the paved walk, passing under Navarro Street.

0.4 Pass an arched stone pedestrian bridge on the left, which crosses the river.

0.5 Pass under St. Mary's Street. Stairs to street level are on the right and a concrete pedestrian bridge is on the left that crosses over the river.

0.6 Reach the floodgates and turn left going up stairs that lead to pedestrian bridge across river to its south side. Back track on the paved path along the river's edge.

1.2 End the hike back at the Alamo.

San Antonio RiverWalk Visionary

It was 1929 and Robert Hugman, a 27-year-old architect from San Antonio, was concerned about the San Antonio River. The flooding of the past several years had left the riverbanks around the Great Bend in downtown San Antonio littered with trash and overgrown with weeds. Deteriorating buildings were above the river level and faced away from it. Most people considered the river an eyesore.

▶

The city hired an engineering firm to provide a solution. When Hugman heard the solution was to fill parts of the river with concrete, including the Great Bend area, he realized the once grand river was being reduced to a flood-control drain. He considered what the area could be if the flooding that made the area undesirable could be stopped. His conclusion was that if floodgates were constructed at each end of the Great Bend, it could be completely isolated from flooding and commercial development could proceed at river level.

Hugman developed a plan called the "Shops of Aragon and Romula." The concept followed that used in cities in Spain, where narrow streets were closed to all but foot traffic. The finest shops, restaurants, and lodging would be there.

Running counter to Hugman's plan was a proposal put forth by civic reformers within city hall who hired a professional city planning firm to develop a master plan for the entire city. Harland Bartholomew's plan for the Great Bend area was radically different from Hugman's. It was to remain natural and untouched, a greenbelt with no commercial development at river level. When the Bartholomew plan was finished and recommended to the city, the Great Depression was in full force. No action was taken on either the Bartholomew or Hugman plan.

In 1936, during the celebration of the one-hundredth anniversary of the founding of the Republic of Texas, Jack White, manager of the Plaza Hotel, recognized that Hugman's commercially oriented plan presented many more business opportunities than Bartholomew's. Using a Works Project Admin-istration (WPA) grant, $40,000 from businesses located along the river, and additional funding from the city, Hugman's proposal was put in place.

Work began on Hugman's San Antonio RiverWalk in 1939, after nearly a decade of debate and delays. Hugman was hired as the architect to oversee the project. He had, through determination, persistence, and endless lob-bying, reached a point where he could implement his vision. It looked like clear sailing, but then opposing social views, differing visions for the city, and politics came into play. Hugman supervised the project for less than one year before he was fired. Despite ongoing controversy between Hugman and city leaders about design and construction materials, the project went ahead and was eventually completed.

On March 13, 1941, the Works Progress Administration formally turned the RiverWalk over to the City of San Antonio. It consisted of 17,000 feet of new sidewalks, thirty-one stairways, and three dams. An estimated 50,000 people attended the dedication on April 21, 1941. The RiverWalk was underutilized for several decades because locals believed it to be dangerous after dark. Hugman established his own architectural office in the Clifford Building on the RiverWalk to counter skeptics that he would be "drowned like rat." Finally, during the San Antonio HemisFair in 1968, the image of the RiverWalk changed, and it was recognized by the world for the treasure it is. Robert Harvey Harold Hugman (1902–1980) is the acknowledged visionary behind that treasure.

San Antonio Parks and Recreation: Mission Espada

The Mission Trail, paralleling the San Antonio River, is the hike for Texas history lovers. It's rare to be able to hike a trail and actually see buildings that were constructed before the American Revolution. The trail linking Mission San Francisco de la Espada and Mission San Juan Capistrano provides an opportunity to not only walk where Spanish missionaries and Coahuiltecan Indians worked, but enter the buildings they used. The church buildings, both constructed around 1731, are the only remaining complete structures from the mission compounds. The Espada aqueduct, built to irrigate the missions' farmland, is in use today, supplying water to a portion of the original irrigation system.

Start: At the trailhead at the northwest side of Mission Espada

Nearest town: San Antonio

Distance: 4.3 miles out-and-back

Approximate hiking time: 2 hours for the hike; add another 1.5 hours to visit the missions

Difficulty: Easy due to the flat paved trail

Trail surface: Pavement

Seasons: Year-round

Other trail users: Dog walkers, joggers, bikers

Canine compatibility: Dogs permitted

Land status: The trails are part of the San Antonio Parks and Recreation Department. The missions are administered by the National Park Service and are part of San Antonio Missions National Historical Park.

Fees and permits: No fees or permits required

Schedule: 9 a.m. to 5 p.m. daily; closed New Year's Day, Thanksgiving, Christmas. Trails are open 24 hours a day, but hiking after dusk is discouraged.

Maps: A general trail map is available on the San Antonio Missions National Historical Park Web site at www.nps.gov/saan. There is no detailed trail map.

Trail contacts: San Antonio Missions National Historical Park Visitor Center, 2202 Roosevelt Avenue, San Antonio, TX 78210; (210) 932-1001

Finding the trailhead:
From downtown San Antonio, take Interstate 37 south and exit right at Southeast Military Drive. Turn left on Presa, right on Graf Road, and left on Padre Drive. Keep Mission Espada on your right; turn right into the parking lot at Mission Espada. The trailhead is near the pedestrian entrance off Espada Road. The mission's address is 10040 Espada Road, San Antonio, Texas. DeLorme's *Texas Atlas & Gazetteer:* Page 159 K9. GPS: N29° 19' 096" W98° 27' 093"

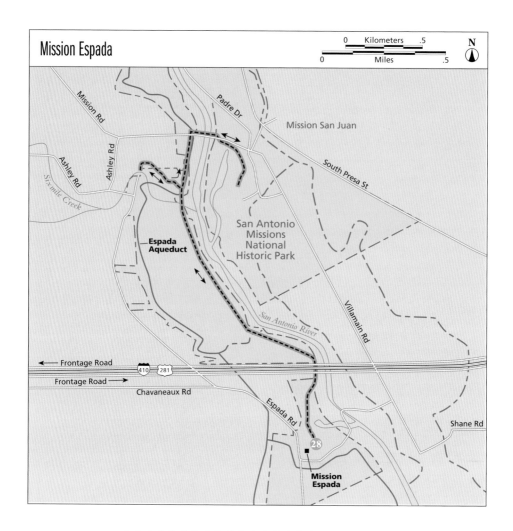

0   Kilometers   .5

0   Miles   .5

N

Mission Rd

Padre Dr

Mission San Juan

Ashley Rd

Ashley Rd

South Presa St

Six mile Creek

San Antonio
Missions
National
Historic Park

Espada
Aqueduct

San Antonio River

Villamain Rd

Frontage Road

410 281

Frontage Road

Chavaneaux Rd

Espada Rd

Shane Rd

28

Mission
Espada

*According to local history, Jim Bowie
and James Fannin are reported to have
taken refuge at Mission Espada in 1836,
before the battle at the Alamo.*

THE HIKE

It's easy to imagine Mission San Francisco de la Espada, located at the edge of
present-day San Antonio, to have been an isolated wilderness outpost. It still
presents a feeling of solitude. The walls that surrounded Mission Espada had
been 10 feet tall and had small two-room living quarters built on the inside for mission residents. People reportedly lived in these quarters as late as 1950.

Prior to starting the hike, look for a large tree about 15 yards southeast of the trailhead and a small ditch. This is an actual acequia built around 1735 by Spanish craftsmen and the mission Indians. There are remnants of a stone water gate that was used to control water flow in the small ditch. To add another dimension to this hike, take time out from walking and tour the grounds, church, buildings, and wall remnants at each mission.

> *The Spanish missions in central Texas flourished from 1747 to 1775, despite repeated raids by the Apache and Comanche Indians defending their territory.*

Stroll through ruins of the San Francisco de la Espada Mission walls and residences. This southernmost of the Spanish missions in Texas was built in 1731.

Start your walk at the Mission Espada on the Mission Trail. Head north from the trailhead; to the left are a few small homes, some having Spanish-style architecture. A large open field is also on the left, which is the same ground that was irrigated by the Espada acequia and used to grow crops for the mission. Portions of the trail parallel the acequia and the west side of the San Antonio River; glimpses of each may be seen.

The area along the hike begins as rural, with the mission grounds on the right, but quickly changes to urban as the trail passes under Interstate Loop 410 and then switches back to mostly rural. The San Antonio River is on the right (east). It was the lifeblood of the missions. Watch for pecan, hackberry, and mesquite trees along the route.

After nearly 2 miles, watch for a spur leading to the Espada Aqueduct. The aqueduct, built in the 1740s, is made from stone and spans Piedras Creek as it carries water from the San Antonio River. This is worth the short side trip and is a great photo op.

At Ashley Road, turn right (east), going up to and crossing the San Antonio River bridge, which has pedestrian and auto lanes. The San Juan mission is on the east side of the river and part of the grounds can be seen from the road. Go a short distance to cross the "old bridge," which is pedestrian-only and crosses over an original channel of the San Antonio River. The mission is directly ahead.

The San Juan mission, with its small church, is still in use as a Catholic church, as are all the churches on the national park's mission grounds. Even though the churches are on park property, they are privately owned. They are open to the public; use respect when entering each church.

Go through the grounds and past the National Park Service office, which may not be staffed. Proceed to the west side of the mission. The start of the 0.3-mile Yanaguana Nature Trail is located here. This is a loop trail with a connector running through the middle. At the trailhead turn right, heading north into the woods. There are observation platforms placed strategically around the sides of the trail.

Follow the north loop around to the connector path and turn left (east), following the path back to the trailhead. At the trailhead turn right (south), passing over a boardwalk. The habitat is excellent for birds. Cardinals and mockingbirds are common, with egrets and cormorants seen seasonally.

MILES AND DIRECTIONS

0.0 Start at trailhead near the center and west side of the mission grounds, where Espada Road dead-ends. Head north on the paved trail.

0.1 Pass under Interstate Loop 410. Continue heading north.

1.0 Cross the footbridge over Six-mile or Piedras Creek.

1.3 Reach a connector trail. Turn left (west) and take the out-and-back trail to the Espada Aqueduct.

1.8 Return to the trail, turning left (north) toward Mission San Juan.

1.9 Cross the Ashley Road bridge over the San Antonio River. Turn right (east) to get back on the trail. Cross over mission grounds, passing the National Park Service office to the west side of the mission grounds.

2.0 Reach the Yanaguana Nature trail trailhead (GPS: N29° 19' 917" W98° 27' 335").

2.3 Complete the Yanaguana Nature trail loop and backtrack to Mission Espada.

4.3 End hike at trailhead at Mission Espada.

> *The missionaries and Indians constructed seven gravity-flow ditches, five dams, and an aqueduct. This 15-mile network provided water for over 3,000 acres of land.*

Friedrich Wilderness Park: Main Loop, Vista Loop, and Fern Del Trail

Perched high on the Balcones Escarpment, this hike becomes exhilarating on the short Fern Del Trail. Go up steep limestone outcroppings, called steps, through a dwarf forest and along a single-track, cliff-hugging path overlooking the canyon. Vista Loop offers a glimpse of the San Antonio skyline. Follow segments of the Main Loop, Vista Loop, Fern Del, and Water Trail to get the best of Friedrich. The golden-cheeked warbler, an endangered species, may be seen during its nesting season.

Start: Main Loop trailhead

Nearest town: San Antonio

Distance: 2.3-mile lollipop

Approximate hiking time: 1.75 hours

Difficulty: Strenuous due to very steep inclines over limestone outcrops on Fern Del Trail

Trail surface: Concrete, wood chips, limestone outcrops, dirt path

Seasons: September to June

Other trail users: Joggers

Canine compatibility: Dogs not permitted

Land status: San Antonio natural area park; San Antonio Parks and Recreation Department

Fees and permits: No fees or permits required

Schedule: 8:00 a.m. to 5:00 p.m. October through March; 8:00 a.m. to 8:00 p.m. April through September; closed Christmas Day and New Year's Day. Park entrance closes one hour before closing time.

Maps: A trail map is available in the park office and online at www.sannaturalareas.org

Trail contacts: Friedrich Wilderness Park, 21395 Milsa Road, San Antonio, TX 78256; (210) 564-6400

Finding the trailhead:

From downtown San Antonio, take Interstate 10 west about 0.5 mile past Highway Loop 1604. Take exit 554 for Camp Bullis Road; this is the second exit past Loop 1604. Go 2 miles on the access road, take a left under the interstate, and an immediate right onto the (two-way) access road. Proceed 2 miles to Oak Drive and turn left. At the end of Oak Drive, turn right onto Milsa Road. Friedrich Wilderness Park is on your left at 21480 Milsa Road. Follow the entrance road to the left to the parking lot and trailhead, which is located near the sidewalk and restrooms adjacent to the parking lot. DeLorme's *Texas Atlas & Gazetteer:* Page 68 K6. GPS: N29° 38' 454" W98° 37' 541"

THE HIKE

This hike combines sections of the Main Loop, Vista Loop, Fern Del Trail, and Water Trail to view the contrast between the flat valleys, dwarf forests, narrow ridge tops, steep hillsides, and limestone balcones found in the park. All trails have signs telling their level of difficulty, from Level One, the easiest, to Level Four, the most difficult.

Start at the Main Loop trailhead, located near the sidewalk adjacent to the parking lot. Pick up a trail map at the sign-in stand near the restrooms, to the left of the trail entrance sign and gate. Follow the concrete walk south and pass a paved area on the left that has a memorial tablet honoring the Friedrichs, after whom the park is named. Mrs. Norma Friedrich Ward, in memory of her parents, gave 180 acres to the city for a natural area; since then, the park has grown to almost 600 acres.

In a short distance the trail branches; follow the right branch, which makes a right turn, going north. The left branch is the Forest Range Trail, which is a paved wheelchair-accessible trail. The concrete surface ends at a three-way branch. Follow the right branch, which is the northern section of the Main Loop Trail. Wood chips, gravel, and then dirt replace the concrete.

A rough limestone trail leads into forests and to stunning overlooks of the valley in the Friedrich Wilderness Park in San Antonio.

Main Loop, Vista Loop, and Fern Del Trail

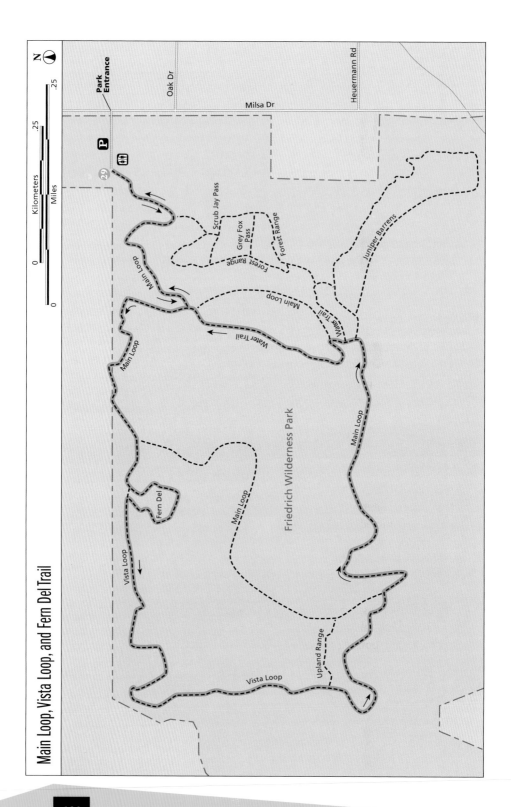

Park Entrance

Oak Dr

Milsa Dr

Heuermann Rd

N

Kilometers

Miles

29

P

Scrub Jay Pass

Grey Fox Pass

Forest Range

Forest Range

Main Loop

Main Loop

Main Loop

Water Trail

Water Trail

Juniper Barrens

Main Loop

Main Loop

Fern Del

Friedrich Wilderness Park

Vista Loop

Vista Loop

Upland Range

Hikers can stroll through wooded areas on many of the trails near Austin and San Antonio.

The trail heads upward and, during a steep climb, passes through a dwarf forest containing mainly Ashe's juniper and blackjack oak. At the top, there is a Y; take the left leg, heading west on the Vista Loop Trail. There are water bars across the trail to divert water runoff and prevent erosion.

Almost immediately there is another branch; go left onto the Fern Del Trail, which is the most exhilarating and strenuous part of the hike. There are steep ascents and descents over limestone outcroppings that the park calls steps. In spots the trail is single-track with sheer dropoffs. Ridges of limestone make good benches to rest on while looking down into the valley, which is covered with ferns and lacey oak trees. The short trail loop starts at the bottom of a north-facing canyon, then climbs about 200 feet to near the top of the canyon and back down, accomplishing both ascents and descents via limestone outcroppings that serve

🌿 **Green Tip:**
Be courteous of others. Many people visit natural areas for quiet, peace, and solitude, so avoid making loud noises and intruding on others' privacy.

as steps. Jogging backpackers use this section as a conditioning workout. There are flat rock ledges near the top, making great benches to rest on.

Complete the Fern Del loop at a T, where it ends and connects with the Vista Loop. Take the left branch, heading west on Vista Loop along the ridgeline. On a clear day San Antonio can be seen from the overlooks. This trail fluctuates from easy to rugged as it follows the top of the hill, drops 350 feet to a north-facing system of canyons, and then climbs back to the top of the hill.

Much of the trail follows narrow rock ledges along the edges of the canyons as it passes through deciduous woodlands dominated by lacey oak, with Spanish oak, cherry, and walnut also present. The forest canopy provides welcome shade. The trail then branches, with the left branch being the Upland Range connector to the Main Loop. A low, stacked limestone wall crosses the trail and what its use was is a matter of conjecture.

The Vista Loop ends when it connects to the Main Loop. Take the right branch, heading south on the Main Loop, passing the connector with the Juniper Barrens Trail. Continue on the Main Loop to where it meets the Water Trail and go left, heading north on the Water Trail.

Highlights on the trail before reaching the windmill are an intermittent creek and a large, seasonal spring. The section to the windmill is narrow and sometimes difficult. Stop and rest on the benches at the windmill, one of the oldest working windmills in Bexar County. Then continue north to meet the concrete section of the Main Loop. Follow the right branch and backtrack to the trailhead.

MILES AND DIRECTIONS

0.0 Start at the Main Loop trailhead just off the parking lot.

0.1 Pass the Forest Range connector on the left (south). Continue on the Main Loop, making a right bend heading north. The Forest Range Trail is wheelchair accessible.

0.3 The Main Loop connector trail T branches with the north and south sections of the Main Loop, and connects with the Water Trail. Turn hard right and head north on the Main Loop trail, following it as it bends hard left.

0.6 There is a Y branch where Main Loop and Vista Loop join. Turn right (west) onto Vista Loop. Within less than 0.1 mile come to where Fern Del Trail intersects Vista Loop on the left (south). Turn left, heading south onto Fern Del. This is a steep, rugged trail, sometimes single-track over limestone outcrops. This is the most difficult part of the hike. This section can be bypassed by continuing on Vista Loop at the intersection.

0.8 The Fern Del Loop intersects and ends, meeting Vista Loop. Turn left and head west on Vista Loop. This is up-and-down hiking. Follow Vista Loop for about 0.25 mile and make a sharp left turn, heading south.

1.3 Pass the Upland Range connector trail to the Main Loop on the left (east).

1.6 The Vista Loop Ts into and ends at the Main Loop Trail. Take the right (south) leg of the Main Loop trail. The trail heads south for a short distance, then turns right, heading west.

2.0 Take a hard left, heading north on the Main Loop where the Juniper Barrens Trail intersects and ends at the Main Loop. Follow the Main Loop north for a very short distance to where the Water Trail intersects the Main Loop on the left (southwest). Turn hard left onto the Water Trail and go southeast for a short distance, then bear right and head north toward the windmill.

2.2 The Water Trail ends, joining the Main Loop at a Y branch. Take the right leg of the Main Loop and backtrack to the trailhead.

2.3 End the hike at the trailhead.

> 🌿 **Green Tip:**
> *Pack out what you pack in, even food scraps because they can attract wild animals.*

Medina River Park: El Camino and Rio Medina Trails

Medina River Park is perfect for nature and river lovers. Start on the El Camino Trail, a concrete, wheelchair-accessible path that goes to an overlook on the Medina River. Pick up the Rio Medina Trail and follow the river through the natural area. The riparian area features large cottonwoods, native pecans, and bald cypress trees lining the river's edge. All the ingredients for a natural area are here, including the river, heavy foliage, wild hogs, maybe a snake, poison ivy, spring and fall displays of wildflowers, and many unusual and colorful birds, lizards, and butterflies. The park is a great place to kick back and enjoy.

Start: El Camino trailhead

Nearest town: San Antonio

Distance: 3-mile lollipop

Approximate hiking time: 1.75 hours

Difficulty: Easy due to small paved section; the rest of the route is relatively flat

Trail surface: Concrete, dirt path

Seasons: September to June

Other trail users: Joggers

Canine compatibility: Dogs not permitted

Land status: San Antonio natural area park; San Antonio Parks and Recreation Department

Fees and permits: No fees or permits required

Schedule: 7:30 a.m. to sundown daily; closed Christmas and New Year's Day

Maps: A trail map is available in the park office. A map may be printed from www.sanantonio.gov/sapar/pdf/medinatrailmap.pdf.

Trail contacts: Medina River Park, 15890 Highway 16 South, San Antonio, TX 78264; (210) 624-2575

Finding the trailhead:
From San Antonio's Interstate Loop 410, drive 4.2 miles south on Highway 16. The park entrance is on the left (east) side just before the Medina River bridge. The trailhead is at the start of a wide, wheelchair-accessible concrete walk, about 90 yards west of the park office. Start at the park office, pick up a map, and head west to the trailhead. DeLorme's *Texas Atlas & Gazetteer:* Page 77 D11. GPS: N29° 15" 300" W98° 34" 421"

THE HIKE

Medina River Park is the city's first natural area park in south Bexar County. In spring, brightly colored birds including painted buntings, indigo buntings, and cedar waxwings may be observed in the wildflower area near the office.

From the trailhead, follow the twisting and turning El Camino Trail. A low stone fence is on the left where the trail makes a gradual bend going right. Pass a large open-sided pavilion that has picnic tables, grills, and a water fountain. A unique feature of the water fountain is that it has a "doggy" fountain about 6 inches off the ground. There is little shade on this section. The Medina River is on the right. The El Camino Trail ends at a cleared area that overlooks the river. Benches, most in shady spots, are placed at intervals along the trail.

At the Y intersection, take the right leg (south) to the gravel-surfaced Rio Medina Trail. The openness now changes to a tree-covered canopy, giving welcome shade. Poison ivy, some bushy and some climbing up trees, is on both the right and left. Underbrush and pecan trees, the state tree, are on a hill to the left, and the right side goes gently down to the river. The bald cypress trees lining the riverbank are unusual in that they have no exposed "knees" jutting up from the water. The rangers have no explanation for this.

Large bald cypress trees line the Medina River. These are notable because they lack the characteristic "knees" that normally appear above the water's surface.

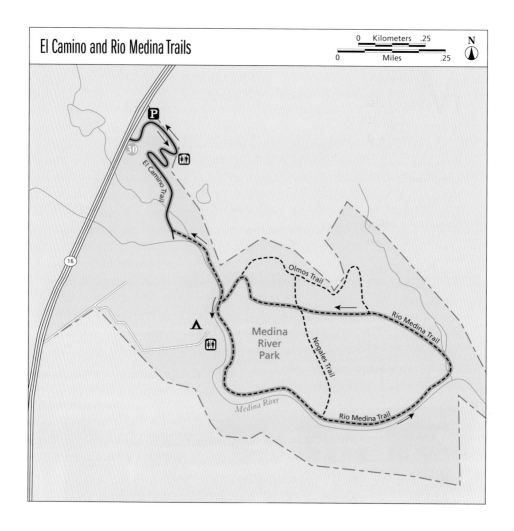

Farther on, a steep footpath goes about 125 feet down to the river, giving hikers an opportunity to explore the river's edge. Pecan trees at the trail's edge keep getting larger, while cottonwoods and hackberries line the river's edge. Pass a path that leads to a spot on the river's bank used as an interpretive area by park rangers. Keep going straight on the Rio Medina trail, which turns to dirt, with the forest and undergrowth getting denser. The trail wanders back and forth, up and down, but is easy to follow. The river heads southwest and is temporarily out of sight.

There is a shallow gully on the right and the left side is flat. Wild mustang grapevines are abundant and many Texans make jelly from the grapes; these are very bitter and acidic, not to be eaten raw. In the spring, wildflowers including gaillardia, winecup, and verbena are in bloom, inviting numerous butterflies, including gulf fritillaries, swallowtails, and sulphurs to gather their nectar. Watch for green kingfishers sitting in tree branches along the river, waiting for an opportunity to have a fish dinner. Follow the trail left and head up a steep grade.

As the trail continues to bear left, heading west, the river makes a right turn going east and disappears. The Rio Medina Trail, which is wide and grassy at this point, continues straight (west). Wild hogs are prevalent; watch for tracks and places where the ground has been rooted up, creating shallow 4-inch ovals that show where they have been digging for food.

Come to a T; the right leg is the Olmos Trail. Stay left and shortly reach the interpretive path that was passed early in the hike. Bear right (north) at this juncture, retrace the Rio Medina Trail to where it joins the concrete El Camino Trail, and return to the trailhead.

The park opened in 2005 and is still developing. It will eventually link greenbelts and trails over a 10-mile area known as City South.

MILES AND DIRECTIONS

0.0 Start at the El Camino trailhead about 90 yards west of the park office at the Medina River Park.

0.4 Reach the Medina River Overlook and the branch with the Rio Medina Trail. Take the right (south) leg onto the Rio Medina Trail, which has a gravel surface.

1.1 The connector Nogales Trail intersects and ends on the left (north) side of the Rio Medina Trail. Continue heading east on Rio Medina.

1.6 The Olmos Trail intersects and ends on the right (north) side of Rio Medina. Continue heading west on Rio Medina.

2.0 The section of the Rio Medina Trail with the natural surface meets the graveled section near the path to the river and the interpretive area. Turn right (north) and retrace the path taken at the beginning of the hike.

2.6 The Rio Medina Trail joins the concrete El Camino Trail at the Medina River Overlook. Continue straight onto the El Camino Trail and backtrack to the trailhead.

3.0 End the hike back at the trailhead.

Hiking Clubs

Central Texas Trail Tamers
www.trailtamers.org

Austin
Colorado River Walkers
JoAnn Fries
P.O. Box 13051
Austin, TX 78711-3051
(512) 480-0291
www.coloradoriverwalkers.org

Fredericksburg
Volkssportverein Friedrichsburg
Joyce O'Rear
P.O. Box 503
Fredericksburg, TX 78624-0503
(830) 992-2053
www.walktx.org

Kerrville
Kerrville Trailblazers
Arthur Bell
P.O. Box 2097
Kerrville, TX 78029
(830) 367-4258
www.walktx.org/KerrvilleTrailblazers

Hike Index

About the Author

Keith Stelter has been hiking, writing, and taking photographs for forty years. His passion for the outdoors has continued to grow since the days he hiked national park trails beside his father. For the past six years he has hiked extensively in the Austin–San Antonio area.

Stelter is a columnist for the HCN newspaper group, which serves the greater Houston area and has a total circulation of 745,000 readers. He serves as the hiking editor–Texas for the radio magazine "Great American Outdoor Trails," a radio show with a listening audience of 4.5 million. The program devotes fifteen-minute segments to hiking in Texas, and its podcasts, along with a weekly Web-based newsletter, are read by over 100,000 subscribers.

Stelter served as executive director of the Texas Outdoor Writers Association during 2006 and 2007. He is a member of the Outdoor Writers Association of America, Texas Master Naturalists, North American Nature Photographers Association, and American Trails Association. He currently resides in Tomball, Texas.